The Fireless Cook Book

A Manual of the Construction and Use of Appliances for Cooking by Retained Heat

Margaret Johnes Mitchell

The Fireless Cook Book: A Manual of the Construction and Use of Appliances for Cooking by Retained Heat

Copyright © 2022 Indo-European Publishing

The present edition is a reproduction of previous publication of this classic work. Minor typographical errors may have been corrected without note; however, for an authentic reading experience the spelling, punctuation, and capitalization have been retained from the original text.

ISBN: 978-1-64439-625-4

CONTENTS

PREFACE

The aim of this book is to present in a convenient form such directions for making and using fireless cookers and similar insulating boxes, that those who are not experienced, even in the ordinary methods of cookery, may be able to follow them easily and with success. The fact that their management has been so little understood has been the cause of failures among the adventurous women who, attracted by their novelty, have tried to experiment with them and have come to the mistaken conclusion that they are not practical, have limited scope, and are altogether a good deal of a disappointment. Such women have made the statement that they are not adapted to cooking starchy foods; that they will not do for most vegetables; that raised breads and puddings cannot be cooked in them, and that there is little economy in using them! It has invariably been found, however, that a better understanding of their management has resulted in complete success, followed inevitably by enthusiasm.

The first few chapters of the book give directions for making and using a cooker, methods of measuring, and some tables for quick reference, followed by a large number of frequently tested recipes, some of which are entirely original, but many of which are based on the well-tried recipes from such books as Miss Farmer's "Boston Cooking School Cook Book," Mrs. Lincoln's "Boston Cook Book," Miss Smedley's "Institution Recipes," and Miss Ronald's "Century Cook Book," somewhat modified and adapted to hay-box cookery. "The Fireless Cooker," by Love well, Whittemore, and Lyon, has furnished some excellent ideas, such as the refrigerating box and home-made insulated oven and insulating pail, which have been elaborated in this book. Miss Huntington's bulletin, "The Fireless Cooker," has also been suggestive of a number of experiments which are to be found in the Appendix.

The chapter on "Institution Cookery" was introduced in the hope that many small institutions, boarding-house keepers, and those who are managing lunch-rooms, would be induced, by finding recipes arranged in suitable quantities for them, to introduce fireless cookers into their kitchens, and benefit by the great saving in labour and expense which is specially necessary to those who are dependent upon their kitchens for support. When a little experience is gained by using them, it will be found that all the other recipes in the book can be enlarged without minute directions.

It will be noticed that nearly every recipe in the book states how many persons it will serve, the idea being that, in spite of the variable quantities which different people use, this would act as a guide to those who wish to plan rather closely. Where two numbers are given the variation is in proportion to the difference between the amount eaten by men and by women.

The Appendix describes or suggests a series of experiments illustrating the scientific as well as the practical side of fireless cookery. Many of them would be easy for the average housekeeper to carry out, and would illuminate the subject to an extent which would repay her; but they are specially planned for students of household economics who have time and opportunity for such work, and who are supposed to know more than mere methods of housework, and to require an explanation of the principles involved.

I

THE FIRELESS COOKER

Does the idea appeal to you of putting your dinner on to cook and then going visiting, or to the theatre, or sitting down to read, write, or sew, with no further thought for your food until it is time to serve it? It sounds like a fairy-tale to say that you can bring food to the boiling point, put it into a box of hay, and leave it for a few hours, returning to find it cooked, and often better cooked than in any other way! Yet it is true. Norwegian housewives have known this for many years; and some other European nations have used the hay-box to a considerable extent, although it is only recently that its wonders have become rather widely known and talked about in America. The original box filled with hay has gone through a process of evolution, and become the fireless cooker of varied form and adaptability.

Just what can we expect the fireless cooker to do? What foods will it cook to advantage?

Almost all such dishes as are usually prepared by boiling or steaming, as well as many that are baked—soups, boiled or braised meats, fish, sauces, fruits, vegetables, puddings, eggs, in fact, almost everything that does not need to be crisp can be cooked in a simple hay-box. If the composition of foods and the general principles of cookery are well understood, but little special instruction will be needed to enable one to prepare such dishes with success; though even a novice may use a fireless cooker if the general directions and explanations, as well as the individual recipes, are carefully read and followed. While such dishes as toast, pancakes, roast or broiled meats, baked bread and biscuits, are impossible to cook in the simpler form of hay-box, the insulated oven, the latest development of the fireless cooker, opens up possibilities that may lead to a much wider adaptation of home-made insulators to domestic purposes. Roast meats, however, may first be cooked in the oven and completed in the hay-box or cooker, or they may be cooked in the hay-box till nearly done and then roasted for a short time to obtain the crispness which can be given only by cooking with great heat.

During ordinary cooking there is a great loss of heat, due to radiation from the cooking utensil and escaping steam. If, however, this heat could be retained, the food would continue to cook in the absence of fire. This is what occurs in the hay-box. Hay, being a poor conductor of heat, will, if closely packed around a kettle of

1

boiling food, maintain, for a number of hours, a sufficiently high temperature to continue the cooking process. The familiar practice of using newspapers or carpet in keeping ice from melting depends upon the same principle. In both cases a material which is a poor conductor of heat, when interposed between the surrounding air and articles which are either colder or hotter than the air, being found to preserve their temperature. Other materials than hay or papers will act in the same way; such, for instance, as excelsior, sawdust, wool, mineral wool, and others. A vacuum will have the same effect as insulating materials. The "Thermos Bottle" and similar inventions, which are glass bottles surrounded by a vacuum and contained in metal cases, will keep foods hot or cold for many hours. If heated with a little boiling water before boiling food is poured in they will even cook some foods satisfactorily. A vacuum is expensive, as it is difficult to obtain, and therefore the ordinary fireless cooker is better suited to every-day use; but if one of these bottles is at hand it may be utilized in cases of illness or on journeys or in other unusual circumstances, when a cooker is not available.

The general trend of recent scientific investigation seems to indicate more and more clearly that the prevalent idea that all food must be cooked at a high temperature, such as that of boiling water (212 degrees Fahrenheit), is a mistaken one. Experiments have shown that starches are made thoroughly digestible at temperatures varying from 149 degrees to 185 degrees Fahrenheit. Cellulose, the woody fibre of vegetable foods, becomes perfectly softened at a temperature considerably below 212 degrees, while albuminous materials, of which all animal and many vegetable foods are largely composed, are not only well-cooked at a low temperature, but are decidedly more easily digestible than when cooked at the higher temperatures of boiling or baking.

SPECIAL ADVANTAGES OF THE FIRELESS COOKER

First, its economy, not only of fuel and of space on the stove, but of effort, of utensils, and also of food materials and flavour. It has been stated that 90 per cent. of the fuel used in ordinary cooking will be saved by the hay-box. This percentage will vary with different housekeepers, as some understand the economy of fuel much better than others, but there is no doubt that it is very great when the cooker is used. This is especially true when the fuel is gas, kerosene, gasolene, or denatured alcohol (possibly the coming fuel for common use). Where a wood fire or, particularly, where a coal fire must be maintained, the fuel saved by the cooker will manifestly be less than with such fuels as can be readily extinguished when their use is over, but even in such cases there is some economy of fuel. One must use the cooker to realize the saving in work that it means. Think what it is to have a method of cooking involving no necessity for remaining in the kitchen to keep up a fire or watch the food! As most hay-box cooking takes a considerable length of time, and many articles are not specially injured by overcooking, this means that foods can often be placed in the box and left for hours, while the housekeeper is enabled to go out for a day's work, or to occupy her time in other ways, with a mind free from all care of the meal that is cooking. The user of a hay-box will soon find, too, that utensils are not so hard to wash after lying in hay as when food has been dried or burned on, and as the scraping and scouring given to ordinary utensils wears them out very fast, there is here also a considerable economy of utensils. There is found to be a very great saving of food materials on account of "left-over" foods and others that might be utilized, if the long cooking which they require to make them palatable did not involve such expense in the way of fuel as to offset the advantage of using them, such as in the case of soup stock, tougher cuts of meat, etc. Special attention is paid in this book to the preparation of a variety of cheap foods and "left-overs."

The absence of heat and odours in the kitchen is another of the advantages of this cookery. On the hottest summer days a cooker will not increase the heat of the room, while even in a living-room, onions, turnips, cabbage, and such ill-smelling foods could be cooked with no suspicion of the fact on the part of the family or visitors. The fact that a cooker can also be made attractive in appearance, and used in rooms not ordinarily used for cooking, is of interest to some people who are not able to command even the ordinary amenities of housekeeping life.

In the matter of flavour there is a distinct gain in fireless cookery. Many are familiar, by experience or hearsay, with the specially delicious flavour of food cooked in primitive ways, such as burying the saucepan in a hole in the ground, of clambakes, or of cooking food by dropping heated stones into the mixture, in which cases the closely covered food is slowly cooked at a low temperature. The praises given to such cookery are often ascribed to the "hunger-sauce" that usually accompanies outdoor cookery, but not with entire justice, for there is a real difference in flavour.

As it has been well proved that tasteless food is less easily or thoroughly digested than food which has a good flavour, owing, probably, to the fact that high-flavoured food stimulates the flow of digestive juices, the advantage lies in this respect also with hay-box food over much of the ordinary food served.

3

The bearing of fireless cookery upon the servant-problem might well fill a chapter by itself. Any woman who uses this device for a year can become eloquent upon this subject. When cooking no longer ties one to the kitchen, is no longer a labour that monopolizes one's time, dishevels one's person, and exasperates the temper, the cook may go. We shall save her wages, her food, her room, and her waste, and have more to spend in ways that bring a more satisfactory return.

DIRECTIONS FOR MAKING A HAY-BOX OR FIRELESS COOKER

The box may be an unpainted one such as can be obtained for a few cents from any store where one of suitable size and shape is used, or it may be a handsome hardwood chest, or even an old trunk. In selecting it, choose one made of sufficiently heavy boards to admit of having hinges and a hasp put on it. If it is to be used in a dining-room, or where attractive appearance is to be desired, it may be covered with chintz or denim, or a coat of paint, if not made of finished hard wood. An old ice-box, one that has a hinged lid at the top, has been utilized for this purpose with success. A barrel makes an excellent hay-box, especially for very large kettles, but the cover cannot easily be hinged and must, therefore, be weighted to hold it down tight. In size the box should be from two to five inches larger in every dimension than the kettle it contains. The kettle is, therefore, the first thing to be secured, and full directions for choosing it are given on page 5. The next point to consider is the packing material. When this has been chosen, the directions for packing the box, given on page 7, will tell how much space must be allowed for insulation and, consequently, of what size the box must be. If it is so large as to admit of more insulation than that absolutely required, there is no objection, only a possible gain. If it is intended to pack the box with more than one utensil this will also have a bearing upon its size. Allow nearly, or quite, double the insulation between the utensils that is provided on the other sides, otherwise there may be difficulty in removing one utensil while the other is still cooking.

Hinges and a hasp, or some device to hold the cover of the box shut, will be necessary, as the packing should be such that there is a little upward pressure on the cover.

A cushion is desirable to cover each kettle used, one which is thick enough to fill the hay-box after the kettle is in place. For making these cushions use muslin, denim, or any thing of the kind that is at hand, filling them, generally, with the same material as that used in packing the box. Shape them like a miniature mattress, joining two pieces which are the dimensions of the top of the box with a strip which is from two and one-half inches to four or five inches wide, the width depending upon the material with which the cushion is stuffed, some materials requiring thicker insulation than others.

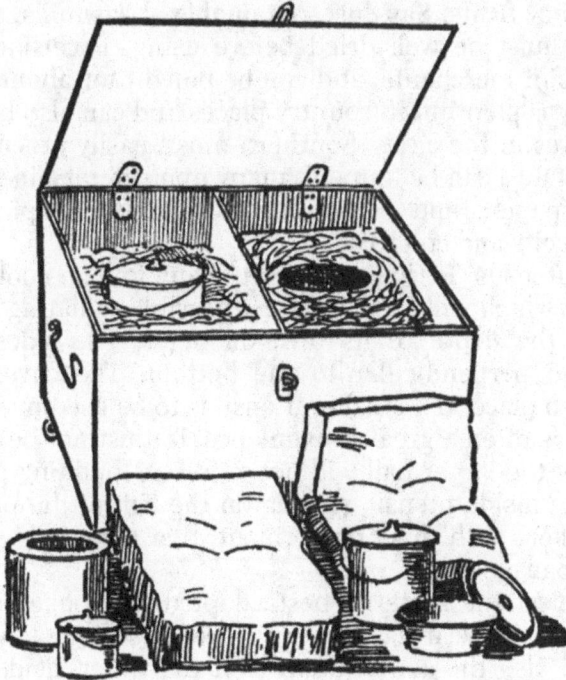

Hay-Box With Two Compartments

Partly packed compartment of hay-box, showing pail in place for packing. Cushion. "Space adjuster." Small pail to fit in "space adjuster." Finished compartment of hay-box. Cushion. Large Pail. Pan and cover.

The packing material may be either hay, straw, paper, wool, mineral wool, excelsior, ground cork, Southern moss, sawdust, or any other non-conducting material that is adapted to filling the space between the kettle and the box. If hay is used, choose soft hay. Wool is, perhaps, the best heat retainer of those mentioned, and it is easy and pleasant to handle. Clean, soft wool may be purchased at woollen mills and elsewhere. It should cost about thirty-five cents a pound, but as it is very light it requires much less, by weight, than of some other cheaper materials. Mineral wool can be purchased at large hardware stores. It costs about five cents a pound, but about five times as many pounds are required as an equivalent for wool. Cheap cotton batting can be obtained at dry-goods stores; ground cork from large grocers. This is used by them as packing for grapes or other fancy fruits. Sawdust, obtainable at sawmills, and perhaps elsewhere, must be well dried before using. Excelsior is used by many kinds of merchants, and can be bought for about two cents a pound. Hay is plentiful in country places and can also be purchased at feed-stores in the cities. Southern moss, easily procurable in the Southern States, can be found at many upholsterers' in the North as well. Newspapers and hair, such as is used by plasterers, are available in city and country.

The utensils. Perhaps the best shape for the cooking utensil, that is, one which will have the least possible radiating surface, is a pail about the depth of its own diameter. The sides should be straight and perpendicular to the bottom. The cover should fit securely into place. If a smaller utensil is to be used inside the large one, which is often a great convenience, it must not be so high that the cover of the larger pail will not go on. A "pudding pan" may be used for the inside utensil, resting on the rim of the pail; but care must be taken, with this arrangement, that a cover is secured that will fit the pan closely.

To select the material best adapted for cooker utensils one must consider its wearing quality, its heat-absorbing power, to some extent, and also the action upon it of the water, acids, salts, etc., which are found in the foods. For instance, iron utensils, as well as most tinware that has been used for any length of time, will rust with the long subjection to heat and moisture; acids will make a disagreeable taste with iron or old tin utensils; while acids in such long contact, with even new tin might also form poisonous tin salts in sufficient quantity to be decidedly injurious. Earthenware would seem ideal except that it is likely to break when over the flame. It is desirable that the covers be of the same material as the utensil, or of some other rust-proof material. It will pay to get the best, when buying these kettles, for they will last well, with reasonable care, and a poor utensil will soon be of no use whatever. Well-enameled iron, except for its weight, is good; also the best quality of agate ware, ordinary aluminum, or, perhaps best of all, for very large utensils at least, cast aluminum. Aluminum is expensive, but its light weight, excellently fitting parts, and lasting qualities commend it above other materials, and it will be found to pay in the end.

The size of the pails will depend to some extent upon the

6

number of people to be served, although there is a minimum size, below which there is not a sufficient bulk of food to cook well. Under the heading "Practical Suggestions on the Use of the Fireless Cooker," this matter of quantity is more fully discussed. For a family of five or six persons a six-quart pail with a pan to fit inside of it has been found satisfactory. It will be convenient to have also a larger pail for large pieces of meat, such as hams.

Method of packing the box. This will vary somewhat with the different insulating materials used. These may be classified as:

Those into which the cooking utensil may be set without any intervening covering, among which are hay, excelsior, and paper.

Those requiring a covering material to keep them in place and to protect them from contact with the utensil, among which are wool, mineral wool, cork, sawdust, and cotton.

Figure No. 1
Pasteboard cylinder to fit the pail.

Boxes to be filled with the first class of insulating materials are packed in the following manner:

Line the box and cover, smoothly, with one thickness of heavy paper, or several thicknesses of newspaper. This will prevent cold air from finding its way through the cracks, and dust and pieces from sifting out. Asbestos sheeting also makes a good lining. Pack in the bottom of the box a firm layer of insulating material not less than three or four inches in depth. This must raise the cooking pail to within from three to five inches of the top of the box. Set the utensil in the middle of the space allowed for it on this layer, and pack around it, very tightly, until level with the top of the kettle. When this is removed it will be found to have left a hole just large enough for it to slip into again. A little manipulation will make the rim of this pocket less ragged than at first. The cushion for boxes packed with excelsior or hay should be at least four inches thick. In packing with paper, lay first an even layer three or more inches

7

thick of folded papers, filling the space around the kettle with soft, crumpled papers. In place of the top cushion, make a bundle of papers folded to just the right size. This can only be done when perfectly flat pail covers are used, unless a supplementary soft cushion be first laid over the pail.

The box is now ready for cooking, but if, after considerable use, the material shrinks so that the whole space is not firmly filled, a little more may be added. There should always be at least a slight pressure when the cover is closed. The paper lining described on page 10, while not necessary to this class of boxes, is an improvement.

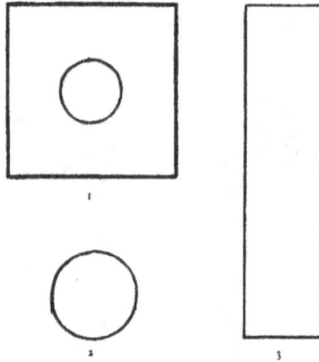

Figure No. 2
Showing how to cut the cloth pieces for lining a home-made cooker.

Figure No. 3
Showing the cloth lining just about to be placed in the box.

Boxes to be filled with the second class of material are packed in the following manner:

Line the box with a smooth covering of paper or asbestos, tacked into place. Pack a layer of insulating material, three inches or more in thickness, in the bottom, laying a piece of heavy paper on this. Sew two or three thicknesses of pliable cardboard into the form of a cylinder that will fit around the utensil loosely. (Fig. No. 1.) It must be of the same height as the kettle. Set this cooker-pail, surrounded by the cylinder, on the layer in the box. Holding the kettle in place with one hand, pack tightly around it, to the level of the top of the pail. (See page 9.) The efficiency of the box depends largely upon this packing. Cut a round hole, the size of the cooker nest, in a piece of heavy pasteboard, to fit the top of the box. Lay this over the packing, so that it will cover it completely. The box is now ready for its cloth lining. To make this, cut three pieces of cloth; one to be one-inch or more larger than the top of the box, with a round hole cut in its centre, one inch smaller than the diameter of the cooker-pail (Fig. No. 2:1); another to be a round piece one-inch larger than the diameter of the pail (Fig. No. 2:2); and the third to be a strip one-inch wider than the height of the pail, and long enough to go around it with an inch to spare (Fig. No. 2:3). Sew the ends of this strip together to make a cylinder. Into one end of this cylinder sew the round piece. The other end is to be sewed into the large piece, taking in each case a half-inch seam. When this is put into the box it will line the nest for the kettle, and cover the pasteboard which rests on top. (Fig. No. 3) Remove the pail and tack this cloth lining in place, turning in the edges where it is tacked to the box. A paper lining may be substituted for cloth in the following manner:

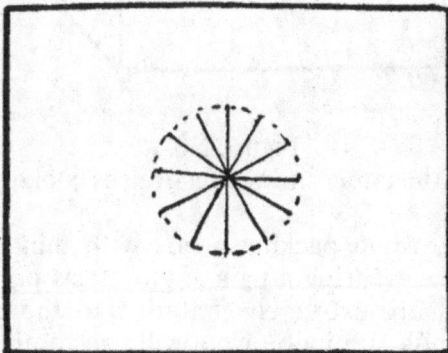

Figure No. 4
Showing the manner of cutting the paper covering for a fireless cooker.
9

Take a sheet of very heavy paper, at least one inch larger in every dimension than the top of the box. Draw a circle in the centre of it the size of the pail. In the centre of this circle cut a small hole large enough to insert the blade of a pair of scissors. From this hole, cut to the circle, so as to strike it at intervals of about one and one-half inches. (Fig. No. 4) Fit the paper over the top of the packing in the box so that this circle will come just over the nest for the pail. Put the cooker-pail into the nest and it will crease the points down at exactly the right place. Figure No. 5 shows the cooker completed. A paper lining is in some respects to be preferred to cloth. It is easy and quick to make and can be readily replaced if it becomes soiled.

With either class of cooker more than one nest may be made. It is well, in that case, to have a wooden partition put into the box before packing it, although this is not strictly necessary. Each portion of the box can then be packed independently and for utensils of different sizes if desired.

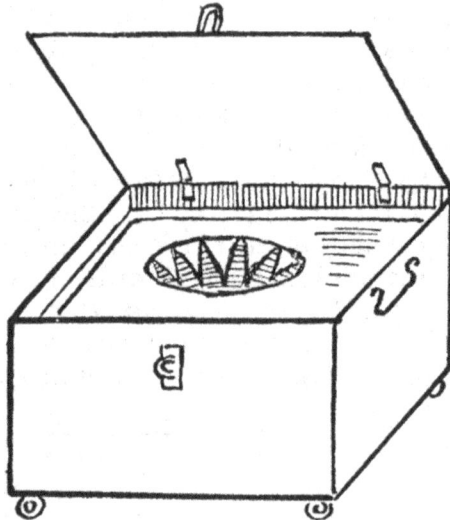

Figure No. 5
Showing the paper lining of a fireless cooker in place.

If possible, when packing a box with mineral wool, do the work out of doors, wearing a pair of gloves, as particles from it fly into the air and are extremely irritating to the throat and skin. Twenty-five pounds of mineral wool will pack a nine-quart pail in a box fifteen by fifteen inches and eleven inches high. Five pounds of wool will pack the same box for using a nine-quart pail. If a smaller pail is used, more wool or mineral wool will be required.

Sawdust is one of the easiest materials to handle. It packs

10

easily and does not require a cloth covering, heavy paper answering the purpose perfectly. Proceed with the packing as for wool or mineral wool and such other materials, omitting the pasteboard top. In place of this and the cloth covering use a paper lining.

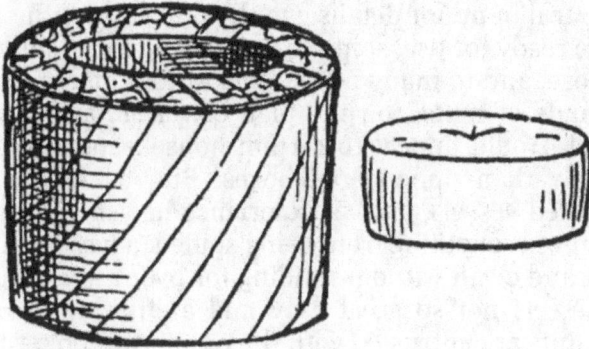

"Space adjuster" before it is covered; and small pad to fill the space below the pail.

The "space adjuster" is a padded cylinder which slips into a cooker pocket and makes a receiver for a smaller cooker-pail than that for which the cooker was packed. It can be made by putting together two pasteboard cylinders of equal length, one of which will fit rather loosely outside of the small pail, and the other of which will slip easily into the cooker pocket and line it from top to bottom. When the small cylinder is stood inside of the larger one the space between the two should be firmly packed, preferably with a soft material such as cotton or wool. To keep the filling in place while packing it the cylinder may be wound with twine, as shown in the accompanying illustration. It may then be covered with a fitted muslin cover. Sew two tabs on this cover, with which to lift the space adjuster out. When slipped into the cooker pocket, and the small pail placed in the new pocket thus formed, there will be found to be a space below the pail, which may be filled by a round cushion made for the purpose.

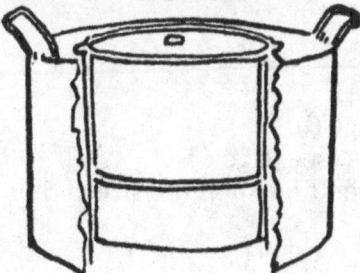

Section view of "space adjuster" showing the pail and cushion in place.

Ready-made hay-boxes and fireless cookers are to be found on the market, some of which have

11

advantages over the home-made article along with some disadvantages. First of the disadvantages is, perhaps, the cost, the expense being considerably greater than for the home-made box. Also the choice in the matter of shapes and material for the utensils cannot be as great as in home-made boxes, and some of the cookers are unpractical in minor details. On the other hand, the commercial cookers are ready for use, some of them being excellently adapted to their purpose, and to many people this would offset the cost. Those that are made of metal, on the plan of refrigerators, perhaps not boxes at all, would appeal to certain housekeepers as likely to be more cleanly than upholstered boxes. But, as food is always in tightly-covered vessels, and as experience has shown that ordinary care will prevent anything from being spilled, a hay-box having been kept sweet and clean without refilling for over a year, the danger of uncleanliness is not so great as would at first appear. Doubtless where servants are entrusted with the use of the cooker there would usually be a greater necessity for guarding against untidiness.

In selecting a ready-made cooker certain points should be considered. See that the parts fit closely together, are simple and strong in construction; that there are no seams or pockets in the kettles which would be difficult, if not impossible, to get clean; that the kettles are a suitable size, namely, not too large, if they are to cook food for a small family, and not too small to ensure sufficient heat for proper cooking; and that there is no air space over the cover that will not be filled when the cooker is closed. In the case of the metal cookers a round cover with a single hinge is a point of weakness, for the cover is not sufficiently supported to endure the strain of constant use. Many of the cookers also use tin very considerably, which is objectionable. Doubtless there will be constant improvements in these inventions, as there is a growing demand for them and an increasing intelligence as to their use.

MATERIALS NEEDED FOR A HOME-MADE FIRELESS COOKER

A box or barrel (see page 3).
One pair of strong hinges.
A hasp.
Material for stuffing (see page 4).
One or more large pails (see page 6).
One or more small pails or pans (see page 6).
Muslin, 1½ yards or more, depending upon the size of the box.
A cooking thermometer.

Heavy pasteboard.
Pliable pasteboard.
Brown paper.
Tacks and screws.

PRACTICAL SUGGESTIONS FOR USING A FIRELESS COOKER

While success in using a cooker is reasonably sure if directions are clear and detailed, and can be followed exactly, yet it is well to understand, in a general way, the conditions of success in order that a deviation from directions, if such should ever be found necessary, will not mean failure.

As the cooking depends upon the retention of heat, it stands to reason that there must be heat to retain. A pint of food does not contain as much heat as a quart, even though both be of the same temperature to begin with. This can be demonstrated by setting a pint and a quart of boiling water side by side. The pint will lose its small amount of heat and grow cold much sooner than the quart, with its larger amount. After an equal time eight quarts of food in the cooker have been found to register 15 degrees Fahrenheit higher than one and one-half quarts, other conditions being the same. This explains the failures of some beginners which are due to the fact that such a small quantity of food was taken that there was not sufficient heat to begin with. Obviously this danger is less with foods requiring only a slight cooking, since, even with small quantities, some time elapses before the food grows too cold to cook at all.

The total quantity of food is, therefore, seen to be an important factor in success. The larger the amount of food, the higher the temperature will be at the end of a given length of time. Where the amount is very large, as in the case of hotel and institution cookery, this gain is so great that the time required for cooking is materially reduced.

The proportion between the amount of food and the size of the utensil in which it is cooked is equally important. Experiments have shown that one and one-half quarts of water, in a pail just large enough to hold it, will register 15 degrees Fahrenheit more than the same measure of water in a nine-quart pail at the end of an hour; while at the end of twelve hours there is 28 degrees of difference. It is thus seen that a well-filled kettle is more likely to cook successfully than one partially filled. When it is impossible to cook in a smaller pail, and thus avoid vacant space in the kettle, the difficulty may, to some extent, be offset by using a pan for the food with sloping sides and broad rim, such as a "pudding pan," which

13

may be set into the cooker-pail and, by resting upon its rim, will be suspended in it. This arrangement admits of filling the lower part of the pail with boiling water or with boiling food, in case a second kind of food is to be cooked for the same length of time.

Space between the pail and packing material is also likely to be disastrous, so that it is notadvisable to try to use a small pail in a "nest" made for a large one without the "space adjuster" described on page 11. Even the space which results after a short use of a newly packed box will be sufficient for the escape of some heat and should always be filled in.

Place the cooker near the stove, since it is important to transfer the food very quickly from one to the other. The cooker should be open, the cushion removed and everything in readiness before the food is taken from the fire; then, before it has time to stop boiling, it should be in place in the box. Loss of time at this juncture owing to uncertain movements is a fruitful source of failure among beginners.

Keep the box tightly closed from the moment the food is put into it until it is entirely done, as if for any reason the box is opened before the appointed time, the contents must be reheated to boiling point before being replaced.

The time for cooking foods on the stove, previous to putting them into the cooker, is usually very short. Food in large, solid masses, as ham, pot roasts, moulds of bread, etc., must be boiled until thoroughly heated to the centre, obviously requiring longer boiling the larger and denser the pieces are. Food that is broken and less compact will be readily penetrated by heat and willbe boiling hot nearly or quite as soon as the surrounding water. Such foods need only a moment's brisk boiling before being put into the cooker. Cereals, although in fine particles, easily settle into a dense, impenetrable mass during the long period of undisturbed cooking, unless boiled until they are slightly thickened.

The length of time for cooking in the cooker depends upon several factors: (1) the kind of cooker, whether well or ill packed, and whether good or poor insulating material is used; (2) the skill of the cook in getting the kettle into the box quickly; (3) the amount, toughness, density, and size of the pieces; (4) whether hard or soft water is used. If hard water is used foods require more cooking to become tender than with soft water. Hard water may be softened, however, by the addition of a little baking soda. The time given in this book is adapted to a home-made cooker, well packed with any of the materials suggested in the section giving directions for packing the cookers. With some commercial cookers a shorter time may be sufficient.

It is frequently stated that few foods are injured by overcooking, but while this is true of a great many foods, it has not proved to be the case with all. Potatoes, rice, custards, raised mixtures, such as dumplings, suet pudding, and brown bread, as well as many other foods, are decidedly injured by overcooking. The recipes generally state the minimum and maximum time which each food should have. This information will also be found easily accessible in the classified index. There is danger in leaving meats or soup stock or even cereals in the cooker long after they have cooled down, as they will be likely to spoil.

Needless to say, careful reading of all the directions given, and following them in every particular, will be necessary until one becomes well acquainted with this novel method of cookery. Mistakes in temperature tests, in measuring, in time, and in other conditions, may result in failures, which must not be imputed to the cooker, but to the cook.

It will probably not be long, after the first experiment with a cooker, before several compartments are fitted up; in which case it is difficult to remember what food is in each and at what time it is to be removed, since it is left for so many hours. To meet this difficulty a slate, hung in the kitchen near the box, will be found a great convenience. It may be permanently ruled and arranged in the form of a table, to be filled out with pencil. A good form to use is the one given below. The compartments may be numbered or described.

Compartment	Food	Time put in	Timefor removal

II

THE PORTABLE INSULATING PAIL

A cheap, portable retainer, for keeping food hot or cold on picnics, automobile trips, and other outings, will be found a great convenience and will fill a long-felt want. Tight-fitting covers, fastened in place, will be necessary to keep food from spilling; and very cheap, easily obtained insulating material should be used for these pails, so that in case the packing becomes soiled it can be discarded without loss. Newspapers, hay, or excelsior are best for the purpose. The object in using such pails is not to cook the food, though this might be done if the inner pail were small enough or the outer pail large enough to allow of sufficient insulation, but to keep food already cooked, or nearly cooked, at a temperature which will make it appetizing. For this purpose a couple of inches of insulation, with such materials as those suggested, will answer very well. If an ordinary fibre or wooden household pail is used, this will carry two or three quarts of food. Take for the inner utensil one justlarge enough to hold the food, and pack the outer pail to accommodate it, like any hay-box or cooker. If designed for frequent use it will pay to make a fitted cushion, but for a single occasion it will not be worth while to take this trouble. Any small cushion or pillow can be used, merely turning the corners under, if it is square. In order to protect it from danger of becoming soiled, lay a number of thicknesses of newspaper over the inner pail before putting on the cushion. Be careful to pack it so that the cushion will fill the upper space completely. A cover must be found for the outer pail, and if a wooden cover is not at hand, a round tray or large kettle cover that will fit it may be utilized. A butter pail, tin pail or candy pail will have its own cover.

To fasten the covers on, tie a loose slip-knot in the middle of a piece of very strong twine (Fig. No. 6:1); before pulling it up tight, slip the noose over the cover of the pail and draw the remainder of the knot out till it is loose enough to go around the pail. If it is placed under the rim near the top of the utensil, or under the fastenings of the handle, it will be held by them from slipping off. Then draw the knot up tight, and tie the two ends of twine over the top. (Fig. No. 6:2.) For greater safety, especially on the outer pail, it will be well to use two such strings, placing the loops at right angles to one another. Soft copper wire might be used for this purpose instead of twine. When the food is in the inner pail, tie on the cover, put it again on the fire until it is boiling hot, and place it quickly in the insulating pail. More than one kettle of food may be placed in the pail if there is room. Food thus insulated will keep hot for hours, even in cold weather.

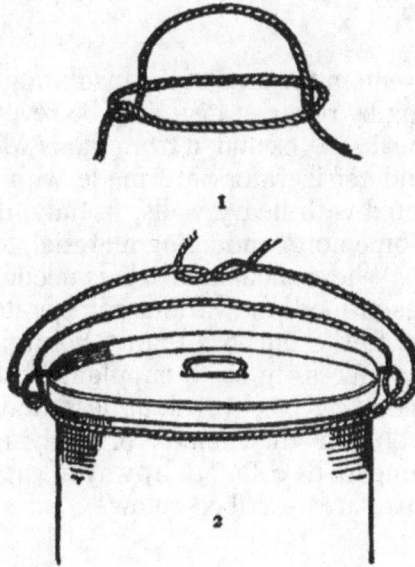

Figure No. 6
1. Method of tying slip-knot. 2. Method of tying the cover on a pail.

Obviously, this arrangement will work equally well in keeping cold foods cool in summer, such as ice water, or cool drinks. Even frozen creams and ices, if packed well in a mould, covered tin pail or can, sealed and surrounded with a small quantity of ice and salt, and the whole thus insulated, will keep for many hours. To seal the mould, dip a narrow strip of muslin in melted fat and lay it quickly over the crack between the cover and mould.

III

THE REFRIGERATING BOX

As we have seen in the case of the insulating pail, the principle involved in cooking by retained heat may be reversed, and the heat may, by similar means, be excluded from foods which are to be kept cold. Ice-boxes and refrigerators are made with this end in view. They are constructed with heavy walls, usually, if not always, with an interlining of some non-conducting material, to exclude the heat of the atmosphere. Where such an article is needed permanently, or for large quantities of food, the various refrigerators on the market are better adapted to the purpose than a home-made box. But, in cases of temporary necessity or to supplement a refrigerator, the home-made refrigerating box will doubtless find a use. Ingenuity will suggest variations in the manner of applying the principle of insulation to keeping foods cold, but by way of suggestion two forms of refrigerating boxes are described below.

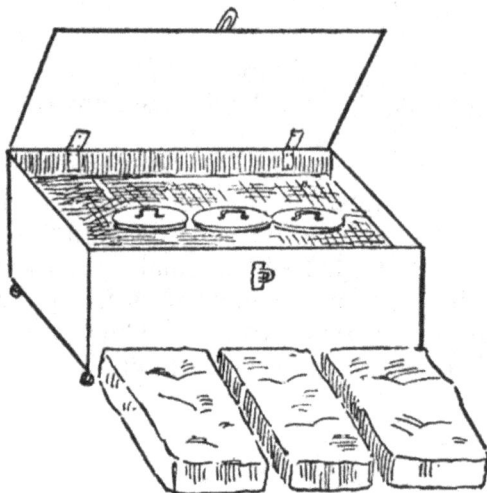

Refrigerating box packed with three crocks

Take three or more stoneware crocks with well-fitting covers of the same material. The size of the crocks must be determined by the quantity of food to be kept. Good results in the way of temperatures have been obtained with those holding a half gallon, but the amount of food accommodated in them is, of course, small.

18

Proceed exactly as for packing a cooker, except that the crocks must be set in place so that all of them touch the central one, which is to be filled with ice.

Although any insulating material suitable for cookers will answer for a refrigerating box, sawdust will be found the easiest to handle, for the reason that its fine particles will more readily fill the acute angles between the crocks, which must be carefully packed or the insulation is not complete. It will be best to make one narrow cushion that may remain in place over the central crock, except when the ice is to be renewed, and two others, each of which can be removed singly when the crock under it is to be opened. Put the food into dishes or pails that can be removed with it and washed. This will obviate the necessity for taking out the crocks frequently and will mean a considerable saving of ice. In lieu of one solid piece of ice, broken pieces will be found to answer excellently. Fill the ice-crock as full as possible, and do not open it until it needs refilling. A little observation of your own individual box will be necessary to tell you just how long your crock of ice will last. It will probably be safe, in any case, to leave it two full days after filling it before opening it. If no foods that have not been reasonably cooled are put into the refrigerating box it is possible that the ice may last three or four days.

Aside from the efficiency of the insulation, the consumption of ice will depend largely upon the amount and temperature of the food in the other crocks and the frequency with which they are opened to the warm outside air; therefore chose as cool a place as possible for the box to stand, and open it only when necessary. Try to think of all the articles you want from it before taking off the cushion. Better results in the way of temperature can be obtained with these boxes than with many commercial refrigerators, although the skill and care in using either will be a large factor in the economy of ice. When it is necessary to open the box, let it be for as brief a time as possible, as every moment that it is open means an increase of temperature and, consequently, a loss of ice.

Another variety of refrigerating box may be made by thoroughly insulating a tin pail partly filled with ice, or a bread box, containing a crock for ice. Allow the same amount of insulation as that called for with the various packing materials used for hay-boxes or cookers, and pack them similarly. It will not often be necessary to remove the inner box if care is taken in handling the dishes of food; but when it is to be scalded, take it out, wash it well, boil or scald it with soda and water, and cool it again before replacing it in the packing.

IV

COOKING FOR TWO

While the fireless cooker is, perhaps, especially adapted to families of average size, or larger, there is no reason why small quantities of food cannot be equally well cooked, provided the cooker is properly made with that in view.

A large utensil will involve a great waste of gas and time, for in every case it will be necessary to heat a considerable quantity of water which is only required to fill the utensil. Select, instead, a two-quart pail, pack it very tightly in a moderately small box, allowing, however, the requisite thickness of insulation (see page 7). This will be suitable for much of the cooking to be done, such as vegetables, steamed breads, etc., that are cooked in much water; but for such articles as oatmeal, stews, puddings, and some vegetables, use a small pudding pan, just fitting into the pail and resting on its rim, with a cover that will closely fit the pan. The pail must always be filled with boiling water or food to touch the upper pan, and if these conditions are fulfilled and the food is put quickly, and while boiling hard, into a cooker which stands close to the range, it will be found to cook as perfectly as larger amounts. Two kinds of food can thus be cooked at once, but, when only water is used in the lower pail, it can be kept in the cooker during the meal, and will be hot when the time comes for washing the dishes.

The fact that almost all the recipes in this book tell the number of persons which they will serve will make the quantity to be cooked easy to ascertain. Where articles are to be cooked in moulds, as steamed breads, puddings, meat loaves, etc., one-half pound baking powder cans may be used. It will be safer to test them to see whether or not they leak. The only change in the method of cooking such dishes that will then be necessary is shortening the time of boiling previous to putting them into the cooker. Small cuts of meat will also require shorter preliminary boiling. One-half the time given will be found sufficient. The great majority of dishes may be cooked as directed in the full-sized recipes, without any change on account of the small quantity.

For such purposes as preserving and baking (see page 101), a large pail will be needed, even by a family of two, and it is suggested that the cooker be packed first to accommodate such a pail, and the box then be made to receive also the two-quart pail by means of the space-adjuster described on page 11.

V

MEASURING

All measurements given in this book are made in standard half-pint cups, tablespoons, teaspoons, quarts, pecks, etc. The dry materials are leveled even with the top of the cup, spoon, or other measure by filling it heaping full, then pushing off with a knife that which lies above the top. When held level with the eyes, nothing should be seen above the cup or spoon, and yet the receptacle should be completely filled. Where standard cups, with divisions in thirds and quarters, are not to be obtained, it will be better to use a straight-sided glass if one can be found which holds an exact half-pint. It will be easier to get an accurate half or third of a cupful in such a measure than in one which grows smaller at the bottom, as most cups do. A cupful or spoonful of liquid is all that they can be made to hold.

Such materials as flour, powdered sugar, mustard, meal, and others, that pack as they stand, should first be sifted or stirred up, and must have any lumps pressed out. Do not shake such materials to level them, or they will settle and the measure will be incorrect. Half cupfuls or other fractions of a cupful of dry material, fat, etc., may be leveled with the back of a tablespoon.

To measure fractions of a spoonful, whether a teaspoon or a tablespoon, fill the spoon, level it, then with a knife divide halves lengthwise of the spoon; quarters crosswise of the halves; eighths by dividing these in halves; thirds crosswise; and sixths by dividing the spoon first in halves, then in thirds across the halves.

21

VI

TABLE OF WEIGHTS AND MEASURES

2 Cupfuls of granulated sugar equals 1 pound
1 Tablespoonful granulated sugar equals 1/2 ounce
2 2/3 Cupfuls of powdered sugar equals 1 pound
2 2/3 Cupfuls of brown sugar equals 1 pound
3 1/3 Cupfuls of bread flour not shaken down equals 1 pound
1 Cupful of bread flour equals 5 ounces
3 1/3 Tablespoonfuls flour equals 1 ounce
1 Pint of milk or water equals 1 pound
2 Cupfuls of solidly packed butter equals 1 pound
2 Tablespoonfuls butter equals 1 ounce
2 Cupfuls of solidly packed lard equals 1 pound
2 Cupfuls of chopped meat equals 1 pound
1 7/8 Cupfuls of rice equals 1 pound
1 Cupful of rice equals 8 1/2 ounces
1 Cupful of raisins equals 7 ounces
2 1/4 Cupfuls of raisins equals 1 pound
3 1/5 Cupfuls of currants equals 1 pound
1 Cupful of currants equals 5 ounces
2 Cupfuls of hominy grits equals 1 pound
2 Cupfuls of samp equals 1 pound
1 Cupful of split peas equals 8 ounces
1 Cupful of dried beans equals 7 1/2 ounces
1 Quart of bread crumbs equals 7 ounces
1 Cupful peanuts, chopped equals 5 1/2 ounces
1 Cupful prunes equals 6 1/2 ounces
1 Cupful dried apricots or peaches equals 6 ounces
1 Cupful macaroni equals 1/3 pound
1 Cupful oatmeal equals 4 ounces
1 Cupful cornmeal equals 6 ounces
8 Medium-sized eggs in shells equals 1 pound
1 Medium-sized egg in shell equals 2 ounces
10 Medium-sized eggs (broken) equals 1 pound
1 Cup almonds, blanched and chopped equals 5 ounces
1 Square Baker's chocolate equals 1 ounce
2 1/8 Tablespoons salt equals 1 ounce
4 Tablespoons pepper equals 1 ounce
2 1/2 Tablespoons ground ginger equals 1 ounce
2 1/4 Tablespoons ground cinnamon equals 1 ounce

VII

TABLE OF PROPORTIONS

Batters; 1 cupful liquid to 1 cupful flour.

Muffin or cake dough; 1 cupful liquid to 2 cupfuls flour.

Dough to knead; 1 cupful liquid to 3 cupfuls flour.

Dough to roll out; 1 cupful liquid to 4 cupfuls flour.

6 teaspoonfuls baking-powder to 1 quart flour, if no eggs are used; or

1½ teaspoonfuls baking-powder to 1 cupful flour.

½ teaspoonful soda and 1 teaspoonful cream of tartar is about equivalent to 2 teaspoonfuls baking-powder.

½ cup liquid yeast equals ½ dry yeast cake, and ¼ compressed yeast cake.

1 cupful liquid yeast, 1 dry yeast cake, or ½ compressed yeast cake to 1 pint liquid if bread is raised during the day.

½ cupful liquid yeast, ½ dry yeast cake, or ¼ compressed yeast cake to 1 pint liquid if bread is raised over night.

1½ teaspoonfuls soda to 1 pint thick, sour milk.

1½ teaspoonfuls soda to 1 pint molasses.

1 teaspoonful soda to 1½ cupfuls thick, sour cream.

½ cupful corn-starch to 1 quart milk for blanc-mange.

1 teaspoonful salt to 1 quart soup stock, sauces, etc.

⅛ teaspoonful pepper to each teaspoonful salt.

2 to 4 egg yolks to 1 pint milk for soft custards.

2 or 3 whole eggs to 1 pint milk for cup custards.

1 teaspoonful salt to 1 quart water for boiling vegetables, meats, etc.

2 tablespoonfuls flour to 1 cup liquid for white sauces and gravies.

3 tablespoonfuls flour to 1 cup liquid for brown sauces.

Whites of 8 eggs make 1 cupful.

3 teaspoons equal 1 tablespoon.

16 tablespoons equal 1 cup.

2 cups equal 1 pint.

VIII

SEASONING AND FLAVOURING MATERIALS

Having always to substitute a familiar and time-worn flavouring, which is in the house, for the newer and particular flavour called for and required to give the distinctive "tang" to a dish, is what gives some people's cooking a monotony that is no easier or less expensive to produce than a variety, if only the kitchen is as well supplied as it might be. Many different recipes can be made, using the same ingredients as a basis, by changing the flavouring, as in stews, cakes, etc. Macaroni and rice admit of a wide range of variation.

For the housekeeper who does not want all her cooking to taste alike, it will be found convenient to have always on hand a variety of flavouring and seasoning materials. A list is given below of the ones frequently called upon in this book; those which are commonly used in sweet dishes being grouped together, and those used in savoury dishes, such as soups, stews, etc., although in some cases these are used interchangeably:

Flavourings for Sweet Dishes

Vanilla bean or extract
Almond extract
Orange rind and juice
Lemon rind and juice
Cinnamon
Cloves
Nutmeg
Allspice
Ginger
Wine

Seasonings for Savoury Dishes

Pepper
Cayenne
Curry powder
Sage
Summer savoury

Sweet marjoram
Thyme
Bay leaves
Worcestershire sauce
Parsley
Celery seed
Celery leaves
Dried peppers

Many of these can be prepared at almost no cost, and put away in tin cans or boxes, either whole or powdered with a mortar and pestle. The leaves of celery and parsley, the herbs and peppers may be washed well and hung near the kitchen stove or in the sun, if they can be kept free from dust and flies out of doors, or put into a warming oven. Orange and lemon rind make good flavourings for puddings and cakes, if correctly prepared, to vary the monotony of perpetual vanilla. The yellow part only of the rind should be grated, for cakes, or shaved off with a knife for custards and puddings, which can be strained to take out the pieces. Caramel is easy to make, and is useful in custards and creams.

To make caramel. Melt one cupful of sugar with one tablespoonful of water, in a frying-pan. Stir it constantly until it is a golden brown colour, add one-half cupful of water, one-half at a time. The sugar becomes very hot, and, if only a small amount of water is added, it does not cool it enough and will be so quickly turned to steam as to have almost the effect of exploding. If the sugar is allowed to become dark brown it will taste bitter. Such caramel is sometimes used to color gravies, but is not sufficiently delicate in taste for flavouring purposes.

Avoid using the same seasonings in every dish. It is better to put only a few flavours together for each dish than to mingle a great many and be obliged always to use the same. It is a good general principle, where several flavours are combined, to keep all somewhat equally balanced so that no one is conspicuously present. Public opinion seems to agree that the skilful cook is the one who makes something good, "but you can't tell what's in it." This is done chiefly by the careful selection and equalizing of flavouring ingredients.

IX

BREAKFAST CEREALS

That so cheap and easy a food to prepare as cereals should so often be unappetizing, and even indigestible, because of poor cooking, is partly due to ignorance of the great improvement in flavour which long cooking gives them, and partly to the difficulties attending such long cooking. No one wants to rise two hours before breakfast to cook a cereal which is advertised on the package to cook in ten minutes or less, and those who do not have coal fires burning through the night are somewhat at a loss to know how to keep cereals cooking over night. The fireless cooker seems to fill a long-felt want in this direction. At the cost of a fraction of a cent for fuel it accomplishes an all-night cooking without danger of scorching, boiling dry, or needing to be stirred. The fallacious idea that boiling temperature is necessary for cooking starches and starchy foods has been proved false. As a matter of fact, a temperature of 167 degrees Fahrenheit is sufficient for the starch grains of some cereals, while long-continued cooking at much below boiling point will serve to soften and rupture the woody fibre which surrounds and entangles the starch and other nutrients. The nitrogenous or tissue-forming substance is probably rendered less easily digestible by boiling, and is perfectly cooked at a temperature which will cook the starches. Merely reaching these temperatures for a short time is not sufficient, however, to produce well-cooked cereals. A further change affecting the flavour, and perhaps the digestibility, is accomplished by long cooking.

The length of time required depends upon the amount and character of the woody fibre, whether the grains are left whole or ground fine, and the degree of cooking they may have had in the course of manufacture. Rolled oats and wheat are steamed to some extent, and do not, therefore, require as much cooking as whole or cracked wheat and oats. Preparations of corn, having more woody fibre than any of the other cereals, will, unless cooked during manufacture, require more cooking than equally finely ground preparations from other cereals. Rice requires the least cooking of all, as it contains the least woody fibre.

Rolled Oats

2½ cups water
1 teaspoon salt
1 cup rolled oats

Look over the oats and remove any husks or pieces. Put water, salt, and oats in a pan, or pail that fits into a cooker-pail, boil them for five minutes, or until slightly thickened, stirring them frequently, then put the pan over a cooker-pail of boiling water and put it into a cooker for from two to twelve hours. Although soft and digestible after two hours, it is greatly improved in flavour by longer cooking. If cooked over night it will need to be heated, somewhat, before serving. This can be done by putting it over the fire while still in the cooker-pail of water. When the water in the pail boils, the oatmeal may be served.
Serves four persons.

Cornmeal Mush

4 cups boiling water
1 teaspoon salt
1 cup cornmeal
½ cup cold water

Mix the meal with the cold water, add it to the boiling salted water; let it boil five minutes, stirring it frequently, then set it in a cooker-pail of boiling water and put it into a cooker for from five to ten hours. If the mush is to be used for frying, use two cupfuls of milk andtwo cupfuls of water, reserving one-half cupful of the milk cold to mix with the cornmeal. When cooked, pour it into a wet bread pan, and slice it when perfectly cold. If coarsely ground meal is used, sift it through a coarse sieve before cooking it, to remove the largest particles of bran. Granulated meal will not require sifting.
Serves six or eight persons.

Hominy Grits

5 cups water
1½ teaspoons salt
1 cup hominy grits

Add the hominy to the boiling salted water, boil it for ten minutes, and put it into a cooker for ten hours or more.
Serves six or eight persons.

27

Cracked Wheat

1/2 cup wheat
1 cup cold water
1/2 teaspoon salt
2 cups boiling water

Soak the cracked wheat in the cold water for nine hours or more; add the boiling water and salt, and let all boil hard for ten minutes in an uncovered pan. Place the utensil in a cooker-pail of boiling water and put it into a cooker for ten hours. Reheat it to the boiling point and cook it again for ten hours.

Serves four or five persons.

Steel Cut Oatmeal

1/2 cup oatmeal
1 cup cold water
1/2 teaspoon salt
2 cups boiling water

Cook it in the same manner as cracked wheat. Serves four or five persons.

Pettijohn's Breakfast Food

21/2 cups water
1 teaspoon salt
1 cup Pettijohn's Breakfast Food

Add the salt and cereal to the cold water, stir until it boils, boil it for five minutes, or until it has thickened, and put it into a cooker for from two to twelve hours. It is improved by the longer cooking.

Serves four or five persons.

Cream of Wheat

31/2 cups boiling water
1 teaspoon salt
1/2 cup cream of wheat

Put all together, stir until boiling, and put it into a cooker for from one to twelve hours.

Serves four or five persons.

Wheatlet

Cook it in the same way as cream of wheat.

Farina

Cook it in the same way as cream of wheat.

X

SOUPS

There are two classes of soup, (1) those made with meat stock, which is the water in which meat has been cooked, sometimes in combination with other materials for seasoning purposes, and (2) those made without meat stock.

Soups made with meat stock include:

Bouillon, made from lean beef, always served clear; or from clams.

Brown stock, made usually from beef, preferably one-half lean and one-half bone and fat, with seasonings of vegetables, herbs, and spices.

White stock, made from chicken or veal.

Consommé, made from several kinds of meat, seasoned highly with vegetables, herbs, and spices, and always served clear.

Broths or beef tea, made usually from lean mutton, lamb, or beef, and not clarified.

Soups made without meat stock include:

Cream soups, made from vegetable or fish stock with milk or cream and somewhat thickened with flour or corn-starch.

Purées, made from vegetables or fish put through a strainer, often with the addition of milk or cream. They also are thickened with flour or corn-starch and are usually thicker than cream soups. White stock also is sometimes used in purées.

Bisques are made like purees, except that pieces of vegetables, fish, meat, or game are served in them in addition.

SOUP MAKING

To make stock. Wash and cut the meat into small pieces or gash it frequently; crack the bone; let meat and bone soak in the cold water while preparing the seasonings; then add the seasonings, boil the stock ten minutes and put it into a cooker for from nine to twelve hours. When cooked, pour it through a wire strainer and set it away to cool. When cold, it should be kept in a refrigerator or other cold place. Be careful that the pail is well filled, or the soup will cool with the long cooking and may sour. If too small a quantity is cooked to fill the pail or pan it should be set over hot water. The cake of fat which forms on top when the stock is cold should not be removed until the soup is to be made, as it seals the stock and keeps out air and germs, thus helping to preserve it. When soup is to be made, the fat is taken off, the stock heated, and any desired seasonings or additions are put in.

To clear soup stock. Remove the fat, taste the stock, and if it needs more seasoning add it before the clearing. Put into each quart of the cold stock the slightly beaten white of one egg and one crushed egg-shell. Wash the egg before breaking it. Stir the stock constantly while heating it. Let it boil two minutes and set it in a cooker for one-half hour or more. Remove the scum and strain it through two thicknesses of cheese-cloth laid in a colander.

To remove fat from hot soup or broth. Skim off all that can be taken off with a spoon. With a succession of small pieces of soft brown paper take off the rest as if you were using blotting paper on the surface of the soup. When no spotted appearance is seen on the papers, the fat is all removed.

To bind soups. This name is given to the process of thickening cream soups and purées, the liquid and solid part of which would separate unless bound together. Melt the butter, and when it is liquid add usually an equal quantity of flour and rub them together till well blended. They are then added to the soup and stirred constantly till perfectly mixed. If the proportion of flour is greater than that of the butter it will be better to add a little of the soup to the flour and butter in a separate saucepan as for making white sauce, and when enough has been added to make a smooth sauce, it may be poured into the soup.

Brown Stock No. 1

3 lbs. shin of beef
3 qts. cold water
1/2 teaspoon peppercorns
6 cloves
1/2 bay leaf
3 sprigs thyme
1 sprig sweet marjoram
2 sprigs parsley
1/2 cup carrot
1/2 cup turnip
1/2 cup celery
1/3 cup onion
1 tablespoon salt

Prepare the meat as directed for making stock, brown one-third of it in a frying pan with the fat. Wash the vegetables, scrape or pare them, and cut them in small pieces. Put all the ingredients together and bring them to a boil. When they have boiled for ten minutes put them into a cooker for from nine to twelve hours. Unless there is a large quantity of soup it is not safe to leave it more than twelve hours, lest it grow cold and sour; but nine or more quarts may safely be left for fifteen hours or more, provided the kettle is at least two-thirds full. Pour it through a wire strainer and cool it as rapidly as possible.

Brown Stock No. 2

1½ lbs. meat and bone, raw or cooked
1½ qts. water
6 peppercorns
3 cloves
½ teaspoon shaved lemon rind
3 sprigs parsley
¼ cup carrot
¼ cup turnip
⅙ cup onion
¼ cup celery
1 teaspoon salt

Do not use salt or smoked meats for soup stock, or any parts of meat which have become charred or blackened in the cooking. Very little of these would be enough to destroy the good flavour of soup.

Cut from the bones all the meat that is easy to get off. Tough ends from steak or roasts should be cut off before they are cooked, and saved for soup or stews. Cut meat for making soup in small pieces. Separate the bones at the joints and crack them if they are large. Soak the meat in the water while preparing the seasoning. Put all the ingredients together and bring them to a boil. Boil them for ten minutes and put them into a cooker for from nine to twelve hours, standing the pan or pail in a large pail of boiling water, unless this recipe fills the cooker pail. Strain the stock through a wire strainer, and cool it as rapidly as possible.

White Stock No. 1

1 chicken or fowl
Water to cover the chicken
Salt (1 teaspoon to 1 qt. water)

Cook chicken or fowl according to the directions given on page 131 for stewed chicken. The water in which the chicken was cooked makes white stock.

White Stock No. 2

2 lbs. knuckle of veal
2 qts. cold water
1 tablespoon salt
12 peppercorns
1/2 cup celery or 1 teaspoon celery seed
1 onion

Prepare the meat as directed for making stock. Pare and slice the onion; cut the celery in pieces. If celery cannot easily be obtained, substitute dried celery leaves, using three or four sprays, or use celery seed.

Put all the ingredients together, let them boil for ten minutes, and put them into a cooker for from nine to twelve hours. Set the pail or pan in a larger cooker-pail of boiling water unless the soup nearly fills the cooker-pail.

Bouillon

3 lbs. lean beef from round or shoulder
2 lbs. marrow bone
3 qts. cold water
1 teaspoon peppercorns
1 tablespoon salt
1/2 cup carrot
1/3 cup onion
1/2 cup turnip
1/2 cup celery

Prepare the meat as directed for making brown stock. Use the marrow fat for browning the meat. Boil all together for ten minutes and put them into a cooker for from nine to twelve hours. Strain the stock through a wire strainer and cool it. When cold, remove the fat and clear the soup as directed on page 31. Serve in bouillon cups with crisp crackers.

Serves fifteen to twenty persons.

Beef Broth

1 lb. lean beef from round or shoulder
1 pt. cold water
¼ teaspoon salt

Wash and chop the meat fine, removing any pieces of fat. Add the salt and let the meat soak for one hour in a cold place. In a small cooker-pail or pan set over a larger cooker-pail of hot, but not boiling water, heat the broth till it registers 165 degrees Fahrenheit. Slip the pails into a cooker for one-half hour. Strain the broth through a coarse wire strainer, remove all fat by the directions on page 31, and serve it immediately in a heated cup; or it may be chilled, or frozen to the consistency of mush.

Mutton Broth

3 lbs. mutton (from neck)
2 qts. cold water
2 teaspoons salt
Few grains pepper
3 tablespoons rice or
3 tablespoons barley

Wipe the meat, remove carefully all skin and fat, as these impart a rank flavour to mutton broth. Cut the meat into small pieces, or put it through a food chopper. Cover the meat and bones with the water, add the salt, and when boiling put them into a cooker for from nine to twelve hours. If barley is used, soak it over night and cook it in a small pail or pan set into or over the broth in the same cooker-pail. When broth and barley are both boiling, put the pails together and slip them into the cooker. Rice would be over cooked if treated in this way, and should be cooked in the strained broth, or separately, for one hour in the cooker. When the broth is done, strain it and remove every particle of fat as directed on page 31.

Consommé

3 lbs. lower part of round or shoulder of beef
1 lb. marrow bone
3 lbs. knuckle of veal
1 qt. chicken stock

⅓ cup carrot
⅓ cup turnip
⅓ cup celery
⅓ cup onion
2 tablespoons butter
1 tablespoon salt
1 teaspoon peppercorns
1 teaspoon shaved lemon rind
3 sprigs thyme
1 sprig marjoram
2 sprigs parsley
½ bay leaf
3 qts. cold water

Prepare the meat as directed for making brown stock, using the marrow fat to brown half of the meat. Soak the raw meat and bone in the cold water while browning the remaining meat and preparing the vegetables and seasonings. Prepare the vegetables as directed for making soup stock, and brown them in the butter. Bring all to a boil together, reserving the chicken stock. Boil for ten minutes, and put it into the cooker for from nine to twelve hours. Strain this stock through a wire strainer, add the chicken stock, and, if it is not seasoned sufficiently, add what seasoning it needs. Cool it as rapidly as possible, and when cold, clear it according to the directions on page 39.

It is served, usually, with custard cut into fancy shapes; or with noodles, macaroni, or other Italian pastes, which are first cooked as directed on page 93; or with delicate vegetables, such as peas or string beans, or other vegetables cut into fancy shapes; or with cooked chicken, cut in dice, and green peas. A poached egg is sometimes served in each plate of soup.

Serves sixteen or twenty persons.

Mock Turtle Soup No. 1

1 calf's head
6 cloves
8 peppercorns
6 allspice berries
2 sprigs thyme
⅓ cup sliced onion
⅓ cup carrot cut in dice
1½ teaspoons salt
2 cups brown stock

¼ cup butter
½ cup flour
1 cup stewed tomatoes, strained
Juice ½ lemon
Madeira wine

Clean and wash the calf's head, reserving the tongue and brains to use for some other dish. Soak it for one hour in enough cold water to cover it. Boil it in a covered pail for twenty minutes with three quarts of salted water and the vegetables and seasoning, and put it into the cooker for from nine to twelve hours. Remove the head; cut off the face meat and reserve it; boil the stock until it is reduced to one quart. Strain and remove the fat from it as directed on page 31; or cool it, and remove the hard fat. Melt the butter, add the flour and stir it until it is well browned; then add the brown stock, one-half at a time, stirring it constantly, and allowing the mixture to boil before adding the second cupful of liquid. To this add the head stock, tomato, one cupful of the face meat cut in dice, and the lemon juice. Simmer for five minutes. Just before serving it add Madeira wine to taste, more salt and pepper, if desirable, custard cut in dice, and egg balls or forcemeat balls. If the soup is prepared, as it may be, some time before it is to be served, slip the pail into the cooker until time for serving. If kept many hours it will need to be reheated.

Mock Turtle Soup No. 2

1 calf's or lamb's liver
1 calf's heart
1 knuckle of veal
Water to cover (about 2 qts.)
⅓ cup onion
⅓ cup turnip
⅓ cup celery
4 cloves
1 teaspoon peppercorns
2 teaspoons salt
1 bay leaf
4 yolks of hard-cooked eggs
½ lemon
Madeira wine

Wash the meat, cover it with cold water in a cooker-pail. Let it stand in a cold place while the vegetables are being prepared. Wash

36

the vegetables and cut them in small pieces. Put them and the seasonings with the meat, bring all to a boil, and boil it for ten minutes. Put it into a cooker for nine hours or more. Strain it, and add to it one cupful of the heart and liver meat cut into small dice. Pour it into a tureen in which the lemon and the egg yolks, cut in quarters, have been placed. Add Madeira wine to taste. The remaining heart and liver may be used for stew or hash.

Serves ten or eleven persons.

Vegetable Soup with Stock

2 qts. brown stock
1/2 cup turnip
1/2 cup carrot
1/2 cup celery
1/2 cup cabbage
1/4 cup onion
1/2 teaspoon salt
2 tablespoons rice or barley

Wash and pare the vegetables. Put all but the celery through a coarse food chopper. Cut the celery in fine pieces. Boil all the ingredients together hard for one minute. Put them into a cooker for three hours or more. If barley is used, soak it over night in cold water and boil it till soft; or cook it in the cooker with boiling salted water for five or six hours.

Cream of Celery Soup

2 cups white stock
3 cups celery, cut small
1 cup water
1 small onion, sliced
2 tablespoons butter
3 tablespoons flour
2 cups hot milk
1 cup hot cream
1 teaspoon salt
1/8 teaspoon pepper

Cook the first four ingredients together in a cooker for three hours or more. Rub them through a sieve; bind the soup with the butter and flour, as directed on page 31, and add the milk, cream, and seasonings.

Serves six or eight persons.

Asparagus Soup

    3 cups white stock, or
    3 cups water in which asparagus has cooked
    1 can asparagus, or
    1 pt. cooked asparagus
    ¼ cup butter
    ¼ cup flour
    2 cups hot milk
    ½ teaspoon salt
    ⅛ teaspoon pepper
    1 slice onion

If canned asparagus is used, drain and rinse it. Cut off the tips about an inch long, and reserve them. Put the stalks of asparagus, stock or asparagus water and onion into a cooker-pail. When boiling, put them into a cooker for two and one-half hours or more. Rub through a sieve, bind it with the butter and flour, as directed on page 31, and add the remaining ingredients and the tips.

Serves six or seven persons.

Tomato Soup with Stock

    1 qt. brown stock
    1 can or 1 qt. tomatoes
    1 onion
    4 tablespoons butter
    ⅓ cup flour
    1½ teaspoons salt

Cook the first three ingredients for one hour or more in the cooker. Rub through a strainer, bind it with the butter and flour, as directed on page 31, and add the salt. Or bind the soup before putting it into the cooker, and strain it just before serving.

Serves eight or ten persons.

Creole Soup

    1 qt. brown stock
    1 pt. tomatoes
    3 tablespoons chopped green sweet peppers
    2 tablespoons chopped onion
    ¼ cup butter
    ⅓ cup flour

3⁄4 teaspoon salt
Few grains of cayenne
2 tablespoons grated horseradish
1 teaspoon vinegar
1⁄4 cup macaroni rings

Cook the pepper and onion in the butter for five minutes, add the flour, then the stock and tomatoes gradually, and cook all in the cooker for one hour or more. Rub it through a sieve, and add the remaining ingredients. The macaroni rings are made by cutting cooked macaroni into very short lengths. Do not soak macaroni for making rings.

Serves six or eight persons.

Ox Tail Soup

1 small ox tail
11⁄2 qts. brown stock
1⁄2 teaspoon salt
Few grains of cayenne
2 tablespoons butter
1⁄4 cup Madeira wine
1 teaspoon Worcestershire sauce
1 teaspoon lemon juice
Flour

Cut the ox tail into small pieces, wash it, drain it, and sprinkle it with the salt, pepper, and flour. Brown it in the butter. Add it to the stock with the vegetables, which have been cut small or with French vegetable cutters. Put it into the cooker for two hours or more. Add the seasonings and lemon juice.

Serves six or eight persons.

Julienne Soup

1 qt. brown stock
1⁄4 cup carrot
2 tablespoons peas
2 tablespoons string beans
1⁄4 cup turnip

Clarify the stock and add the cooked beans and peas and the carrot and turnip, which have been cut into thin strips one and one-half inches long and cooked for two hours in the cooker. When boiling hot, serve it.

Serves four or five persons.

Macaroni Soup

1 qt. brown stock
1/4 cup macaroni rings

Cook the macaroni in boiling salted water for two hours in the cooker. Drain it in a colander. Cut it into very short lengths to make rings. Heat them in the stock.

SOUPS MADE WITHOUT STOCK

Vegetable Soup

1/3 cup carrot
1/3 cup turnip
1/2 cup celery
1/2 cup onion
11/2 cups potato
1 pt. tomatoes
5 tablespoons butter
1/2 tablespoon parsley
2 teaspoons salt
1/4 teaspoon pepper
1 qt. water

Wash the vegetables, scrape the carrot, pare the turnip, potatoes, and onions, remove the leaves and strings from the celery, and cut the vegetables in small pieces, or put all except the potatoes and celery through a coarse food chopper. Measure the vegetables after they are prepared. Put them all, except the potatoes and parsley, into a frying pan with the butter, and cook them for ten minutes; add the potatoes and cook them for two minutes more, then put all the ingredients, except the parsley, together in a cooker-pail, and when they are boiling put them into a cooker for three hours or more. Add the parsley just before serving. "Left-over" vegetables, in pieces, may be added, in place of an equal measure of any of the first five given.

Serves six or eight persons.

Bean Soup

1 pt. beans
2 qts. water or stock
1 onion
1/2 lb. lean, raw beef, if stock is not used
2 tablespoons Chili sauce
2 tablespoons butter
2 tablespoons flour
2 1/2 teaspoons salt
1/4 teaspoon pepper
2 stalks celery

Wash and soak the beans over night, cut the meat small, and pan-broil the pieces in a dry, hot frying pan till brown. Put all the ingredients except the butter and flour into a cooker-pail, and when they are boiling put them into a cooker for from nine to twelve hours. Rub the soup through a strainer, and bind it.

Serves eight or ten people.

Black Bean Soup

1 pt. black beans
2 qts. water
1 small onion
2 stalks celery, or
1/4 teaspoon celery salt
2 teaspoons salt
1/8 teaspoon pepper
1/4 teaspoon mustard
Cayenne
3 tablespoons butter
1 1/2 tablespoons flour
2 hard-cooked eggs
1 lemon

Soak the beans over night, drain them and add the two quarts of water. Cook the onion in one-half of the butter; add onion and celery to the beans, and, when boiling, put them into a cooker for from eight to twelve hours. Rub the soup through a strainer, add the seasonings, bind it, and when it has boiled for five minutes pour it over the sliced eggs and lemon in a soup tureen.

Serves eight or ten persons.

41

Tomato Soup

1 can tomatoes, or
1 qt. raw tomatoes
1 pt. water
12 peppercorns
1 small bay leaf
4 cloves
1 slice onion
2 teaspoons salt
1/8 teaspoon soda
2 teaspoons sugar
2 tablespoons butter
3 tablespoons flour

Cook the first six ingredients together in a cooker for one hour or more. Strain, add the salt and soda, and bind it. If it is not to be served at once it may stand in the cooker, to keep hot, for an indefinite period.

Serves six or seven persons.

Purée of Lima Beans

1 cup dried lima beans
3 pts. water
2 slices onion
2 slices turnip
1 cup cream or milk
4 tablespoons butter
2 tablespoons flour
2 teaspoons salt
1/4 teaspoon pepper

Wash the beans and soak them over night. Drain them, and, when boiling, cook them with the prepared onion and turnip and the water in a cooker for four hours or more. Rub this through a strainer, add the seasoning and cream or milk, and bind it.

Serves seven or nine persons.

Baked Bean Soup

3 cups cold baked beans
3 pints water
2 slices onion

2 stalks celery
1½ cups tomato
2 tablespoons butter
2 tablespoons flour
1 tablespoon Chili sauce
1 teaspoon salt
⅛ teaspoon pepper

Cook the first five ingredients in a cooker for three hours or more, rub them through a strainer, bind this with the butter and flour, as directed on page 31, and add the seasonings.

Serves eight or ten persons.

Green Pea Soup

1 can marrowfat peas, or
1 pt. shelled peas
2 teaspoons sugar
1 pt. water
1 pt. milk
1 slice onion
2 tablespoons butter
2 tablespoons flour
1½ teaspoon salt
⅙ teaspoon pepper

If fresh peas are used take those which are too old to be good to serve as a vegetable. If canned peas are used, drain and rinse them, add the sugar, water, and onion, and, when boiling, put them into a cooker for two hours or more. Rub them through a strainer, add the hot milk and seasoning and bind the soup with the butter and flour, as directed on page 31.

Bean and pea soups are very nourishing and should not be followed by a rich, hearty meal.

Serves five or six persons.

Potato Soup

3 potatoes
1 pt. milk
1 pt. water
2 slices onion

4 tablespoons butter
2 tablespoons flour
1½ teaspoons salt
¼ teaspoon celery salt
⅛ teaspoon pepper
Cayenne
1 teaspoon chopped parsley

Scrub and pare the potatoes and cut them into small pieces. Cook them in a cooker with the water and onion for one and one-half hours or more, standing the pail or pan in a larger cooker-pail of boiling water. Rub the soup through a sieve, bind it, and add the seasoning.

Serves five or six persons.

Fish Chowder

4 lbs. cod, haddock, or other firm white fish
4 cups potatoes (in ¾ inch dice)
1 onion, sliced
4 cups scalded milk
1½ inch cube fat salt pork
1 tablespoon salt
⅛ teaspoon pepper
3 tablespoons butter
⅔ cup oyster crackers

Skin the fish (see page 49), cut the flesh into two-inch pieces, put the head, tail, and bones into a small cooker-pail or pan, add two cups of cold water and bring it to a boil. Set this into a larger cooker-pail of boiling water to which one teaspoonful of salt has been added for each quart of water. Put the potatoes in this lower pail and, when boiling, cook all in the cooker for one hour.

Cut the pork into small pieces, try out the fat in a frying-pan and fry the onion in it. When the fish and potatoes are cooked, drain off the fish-liquor, add all the ingredients except the milk and crackers to it, bring it to a boil and place it in the cooker for one-half hour. Add the milk and pour the chowder over the crackers in a tureen.

Serves twelve or sixteen persons.

Connecticut Chowder

Make this in the same manner as fish chowder, substituting

44

two and one-half cups of stewed or canned tomatoes for the milk. The tomatoes may be added to the other ingredients when they are put together. If desired, crumble the crackers and add them just before serving.

Serves ten or twelve persons.

Clam Chowder

1/2 pk. clams in the shell or 1 qt. clams
1 qt. potatoes, cut in 3/4 inch dice
1 cup water
11/2 inch cube fat salt pork
1 tablespoon salt
1/8 teaspoon pepper
4 tablespoons butter
1 qt. scalding hot milk, or
6 or 8 soda crackers, broken or crumbled
21/2 cups stewed tomatoes

Wash the clams in a strainer, pick them over, to see that there are no bits of shell with them, and cut off the soft parts. Chop the hard parts or cut them into small pieces. Cut the pork into pieces, try out the fat, and fry the onion in it. Put all the ingredients together, except the crackers and the milk, if that be used, into a cooker-pail. Bring them to a boil and put them into the cooker for from one to two hours. Reheat the soup and add the milk and crackers.

Serves ten to sixteen persons.

Split-pea Soup

1 pt. split peas
1 soup bone (2 lbs.)
2 qts. cold water
23/4 teaspoons salt
1/4 teaspoon pepper

Soak the peas over night and drain them. Wash the bone, boil it for ten minutes in the water and skim it, add the peas and seasoning, bring all to a boil and put it into the cooker for four hours or more. Take out the bone and serve the soup without straining it. The peas must be cooked until they fall to pieces easily when well beaten. If desired, the meat may be taken from the bone, cut into small pieces and served in the soup.

Oyster or Clam Stew

1 qt. oysters or clams
1 qt. milk
1/4 cup butter
1 1/2 tablespoons salt
1/6 teaspoon pepper

Heat the milk till it boils. Heat the oysters or clams in their liquor which has been strained through cheese-cloth. Add the pepper and the hot milk and put the stew at once into a cooker for one-half hour or more. Oysters will keep for some hours without curdling if they do not boil after the milk is added and if the salt is put in just before serving. It will be safer to keep the clams and milk separate while in the cooker and combine them just before serving. Less salt will be needed for clams than for oysters.

SOUP GARNISHES

Noodles

1 egg
1/2 teaspoon salt
Flour to make a stiff dough

Beat the egg until it is evenly mixed, add a little flour, through which the salt has been mixed. Gradually add more flour until a dough is made that can be rolled out very thin. Knead it a few minutes, then roll it as thin as possible. Let it stand for fifteen or twenty minutes covered with a towel, then roll it like jelly-roll and cut, from the end of the roll, very narrow slices. Unroll these strips and lay them on a board, covered lightly with a towel or clean cloth, to dry. When perfectly dry they are ready to use, or may be put away in covered cans or boxes and kept in a cool place.

If noodles are used as a vegetable they should be prepared as macaroni, except that they must not be soaked before cooking.

Egg Balls

4 eggs, cooked
1 egg, raw
1/2 teaspoon salt
1 teaspoon butter
1/8 teaspoon pepper

46

Put the eggs into enough cold water to more than cover them (at least one quart for every four eggs), bring this to a boil and put it into a cooker for twenty minutes. Drop the eggs into cold water, take off the shells and when they are cold carefully remove the whites, leaving the yolks whole. These may be dropped into soup as they are, or they may be mashed, mixed with the butter and salt and enough egg yolk, or egg white or whole egg, beaten, to moisten them, so that they may be moulded into balls about the size of a hard-cooked yolk. Roll these in flour and sauté them in butter.

Forcemeat Balls

¼ cup fine, soft crumbs
¼ cup milk
1 teaspoon salt
1 egg
2/3 cup raw fish or meat
1 tablespoon flour
1 tablespoon butter

Cook the bread and milk to a paste, cool it, add the beaten egg and fish or meat, forced through a fine meat-chopper or chopped and then ground fine with a mortar and pestle. Mould it into balls, lay them in a pan with the flour and shake it until the balls are floured; then sauté them with the butter, shaking the pan carefully from time to time, till the balls are browned on all sides. Or the balls may be dropped into boiling soup and put into the cooker for one-half hour.

Croûtons

Cut slices of bread one-half inch thick, spread thinly with butter. Cut the slices into strips one-half inch wide, and these into dice one-half inch thick. Put them into a baking-pan, and brown them in a hot oven, stirring them about frequently that they may be brown evenly. Add them to the soup just before serving, or pass them after serving.

Soup Sticks

Prepare the bread exactly as for croûtons, except that the strips of bread are not cut into dice. If desired the strips may be sprinkled with grated cheese after they are cut. Lay them side by side with enough space between them to allow them to brown on the sides. Serve them as an accompaniment to soup.

Crisp Crackers

Split plain, thick crackers; spread the rough sides slightly with butter, and brown them delicately in a hot oven.

XI

FISH

To tell fresh fish. The flesh of fresh fish is firm, and will rise quickly if pressed with the finger; the eyes are bright, and the gills red. Frozen fish may be kept for a long time, but must be used at once when thawed, as it spoils more quickly than fresh fish. Thaw frozen fish in cold water.

Care of fish. Clean it and wipe it, inside and out, with a cloth dipped in strongly salted water. Do not put steaks or cutlets of fish into the water. Lay it on a plate on cracked ice, or in a cool place. It must not be kept in an ice-box unless wrapped in two thicknesses of brown paper, or it will impart an odour to milk, butter, and other foods.

To clean a fish. Before opening it remove the scales by scraping slowly from the tail toward the head, holding the knife nearly flat on the fish. Rinse the knife frequently in cold water. Open the fish on the under side, cutting a slit from the gills half-way down the body. Removethe entrails clear to the backbone, scraping the inside if necessary.

To skin a fish. Cut a slit down the back to the tail, on both sides of the dorsal fins, deep enough to take them out. Insert a sharp-pointed knife under the skin as near the gills as possible. Holding the head by the bony part near the gills, work the knife down toward the tail.

Cooking of fish. Fish is sufficiently cooked when the flesh will easily flake away from the bones. If boiled too long, it becomes soft and watery. An acid flavour is palatable with fish, and for this reason slices of lemon or an acid sauce are often served with it.

Left-over boiled fish may be served in a variety of ways, as creamed fish, scalloped fish, fish soufflé, croquettes, casserole of fish, etc.

TABLE OF THE SEASONS, ETC., OF FRESH-WATER FISH

NAME OF FISH	WEIGHT	IN SEASON
Salmon	5 or 6 lbs., or more	May to Sept.
Shad	3 lbs., or more	Jan. to June
White fish	4 lbs.	Winter

Bass	3 to 8 lbs.	Always
Perch	Average 8 to a lb.	Summer
Pickerel	1 to 4 lbs.	Always
Brook Trout		Apr. to Aug.
Lake Trout	4 to 9 lbs.	Apr. to Aug.
Pike		Summer

TABLE OF SEASONS, ETC., OF SALT-WATER FISH

NAME OF FISH	WEIGHT	IN SEASON
Cod	3 to 20 lbs.	Always
Haddock	5 to 8 lbs.	Always
Black Bass	3 lbs.	Aug. to Mar.
Cusk	5 to 8 lbs.	Winter
Halibut		Always
Flounders	½ to 5 lbs.	Always
Red snapper	4 lbs., or more	Late winter
Bluefish	4 to 8 lbs.	June to Oct.
Tautog		July to Sept.
Sturgeon		Summer
Swordfish		July to Sept.
Weakfish	3 to 5 lbs.	Winter
Mackerel	¾ to 2 lbs.	May to Sept.
Turbot		Jan. to Mar.
Herring	6 or 8 to a lb.	Mar. and Apr.
Smelts	Average 8 to a lb.	Sept. to Mar.
Lobsters	1 to 2 lbs.	Always
Oysters		Sept. to May
Clams		Always
Crabs		Summer

Boiled Fish

Put a three-pound fish, or three pounds of small fish, into four quarts of boiling water to which four teaspoonfuls of salt have been added. Set it at once into the cooker for one hour. Larger fish may be cooked in the same way if more water is used. For instance, a four-pound fish should be put into five or six quarts of water. Or, with large fish, put them into boiling water to cover them, let them come to a boil, and put them into the cooker for three-quarters of an hour or more, according to the size of the fish. Fish when overcooked will be watery, but will not break to pieces, unless very much overdone, if cooked in a hay-box or cooker.

Creamed Salt Codfish No. 1

1 lb. fish
3 or 4 qts. Water

Wash the fish and, without shredding it, put it into the cold water, bring it to a boil, and put it into a cooker for one and one-half hours. Drain, pick into pieces, and bring to a boil in one cup of white sauce, omitting the salt. It is improved by adding a beaten egg before serving.
Serves six or seven persons.

Creamed Salt Codfish No. 2

1 lb. codfish
3 or 4 qts. water
1/4 cup butter
4 eggs
1/2 cup milk
1/8 teaspoon pepper

Cook the fish as for creamed salt codfish No. 1. When picked to pieces, put it into a double boiler with the butter. When this is absorbed by the fish add the remaining ingredients beaten together. Cook, stirring constantly, until it thickens like custard. Serve at once or it will curdle.
Serves six or eight persons.

Codfish Balls

1 cup raw salt codfish, in small pieces
1 heaping pint potatoes in 1-inch pieces
3 qts. cold water
1 egg
1/2 tablespoon butter
1/8 teaspoon pepper

51

Bring the fish and potatoes to a boil in the water. Put them into a hay-box for one and one-half hours. Drain and shake them, uncovered, over the fire to dry them as boiled potatoes, till white and mealy. Mash them thoroughly, add the other ingredients, and mix them together thoroughly. If necessary, add a little more salt. Take the mixture up by tablespoonfuls and, without moulding them, drop them into hot, deep fat. Fry until they are a rich brown, and drain them on brown paper.

To test the temperature of fat for fish balls, drop a cube of stale bread into the fat. If it grows a rich brown in forty seconds the fat is of the right temperature. If fat is too hot, fried food is injured in flavour and digestibility; if not hot enough the food will be greasy. If fish balls fall apart in the frying, it is because the fish and potatoes were not well dried before adding the other ingredients.

Serves four or six persons.

Salt Fish Soufflé

1 cup salt codfish
1 heaping pt. potatoes
3 qts. water
2½ tablespoons butter
7⁄8 cup milk
1⁄8 teaspoon pepper
2 eggs

Cook the fish and potatoes as for codfish balls. When drained and dried, add the butter, milk, pepper, and yolks of eggs; then the whites, beaten stiff. Turn into a buttered baking-dish, and bake until puffed and brown (about one-half hour) in an insulated oven, the stones heated until the paper test shows a golden brown.

Serves eight or ten persons.

Salmon Loaf

1 can salmon
1⁄4 cup butter (melted)
1 cup soft breadcrumbs
4 eggs
1⁄8 teaspoon pepper
1½ teaspoons salt
2 tablespoons chopped parsley
1 small bay leaf

If only hard, dry crumbs can be obtained, add one-fourth of a cup of water to the recipe, mixing it with the eggs, and soaking the crumbs one-half hour in the mixture.

Rub the fish and butter together, add the other ingredients, and put all into a buttered one-quart bread-mould or water-tight empty coffee or baking-powder can. Set the mould in enough cold water to reach two-thirds of the way up its sides. Let this come to a boil, boil fifteen minutes and put into the cooker for one hour. It will not be injured by remaining in the hay-box two hours. Or set the mould into boiling water, boil one-half hour, and put into the cooker for an hour.

Serves eight or ten persons.

Casserole of Fish

1 cup cold flaked fish
1 teaspoon salt
1 cup mashed potatoes
2 hard-cooked eggs
1/8 teaspoon pepper

Butter a quart mould, put into it alternate layers of fish, potatoes, and egg; seasoning each layer. Stand the mould in a cooker-pail of boiling water to reach two-thirds of the way up its sides. Boil ten minutes and put it into the cooker for from three-quarters of an hour to two hours.

Serves six persons.

Cape Cod Turkey

1 lb. salt codfish
4 qts. cold water
1/4 lb. fat salt pork

Wash the fish and put it on the stove in the water. When boiling, put it into a cooker and let it cook from one and one-half to three hours. While this is cooking cut the pork into one-fourthinch slices, gash the slices occasionally, nearly to the rind. Pour boiling water over it, drain it, and try it out in a frying-pan till brown and crisp. When the codfish is done, drain it and garnish it with a border of the hot, crisp pork. Serve drawn-butter sauce and boiled potatoes with it.

Serves six or eight persons.

Creamed Oysters

1 qt. oysters
2 cups milk or cream
1/4 cup butter
1/4 cup flour
3/4 teaspoon salt
Few grains of white pepper

Drain and wash the oysters. Strain the liquor through cheese-cloth. Heat the oysters in the liquor by themselves and scald the milk. Rub the butter and flour together, add them to the hot milk or cream, and let it boil. Put this mixture with the boiling oysters and set it in a cooker for one-half hour or more. Just before serving add the seasoning. Serve it on toast or crisped crackers, or in croustades.

XII

BEEF

To select good beef. (1) Quality. "Heavy" beef, that is, taken from fat, heavy animals, is the best. It should be mottled with fat all through the lean, and the large masses of fat should be firm and of a creamy white colour. The grain of tender meat is fine. Coarse-grained meat, and meat streaked with connective tissue or gristle, is sure to be tough. (2) Freshness. Fresh beef is a good red colour, modified, when it is very cold, to a purplish shade. If black or greenish in tint the meat is stale, and its odour will be bad. Meat is flabby after it is killed, but soon grows firm. It is in suitable condition for cooking before this change takes place, or some days after it.

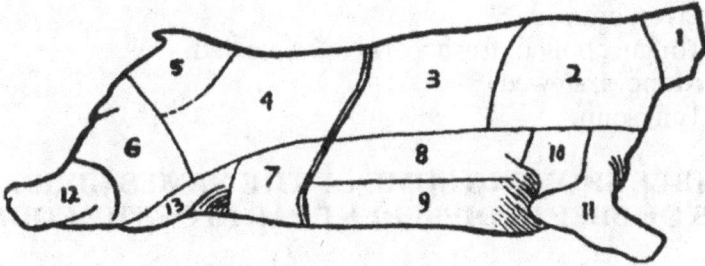

Figure No. 7
Diagram of the cuts of beef. The double line shows the division between forequarter and hindquarter.

Uses of the different cuts. Beef is cut variously in different parts of the country, and the same cuts are not always similarly named. Merely to call the cuts by name would, therefore, make this chapter unintelligible to some readers; but by consulting the accompanying chart the pieces can be selected without reference to their names, according to the part of the animal adapted to each particular use. Those muscles which are much used and which have hard work to do will have the most juice and the best flavour, though, at the same time, they will be the toughest. For instance, all cuts, such as round, shoulder, shin, and rump, which come from the legs or parts by which the legs are connected with the body, will be tough and high-flavoured. The neck also, and upper part of the shoulder, by reason of the support they give to the weight of the head, are tough, although rich in flavour. Any cuts from these parts, by whatever name they are called, are not suitable for cooking with dry heat, such as that of baking, or broiling, but will require long, slow cooking with water to make them tender. Such pieces are the ones to buy for cooking in a hay-box. They do not command the price of the tender cuts from the back of the animal, and it is, therefore, a distinct economy to buy these cheap pieces and by skilful cooking make them digestible and palatable. The parts numbered 1, 2, 7, 8, 9, in Fig. 7 are suitable for stews; those marked 11 and 12, as well as all bones, are suitable for soups. Numbers 2, 5, 6, and 10 may be used for stews or broth, but are adapted also to pot roasts, rolled steaks, cannelon, Hamburg steak, etc., while only numbers 3 and 4 are adapted to roasting or broiling.

Other parts of beef used as food, suitable for cooking in the hay-box or cooker, are:

Brains, stewed or scalloped, or for croquettes.

Heart, stuffed and braised.

Liver, braised.

Tongue, boiled; fresh, corned, or pickled.

Kidneys, stewed.

Tail, soup.

TABLE SHOWING SOME OF THE NAMES GIVEN TO CUTS OF BEEF IN DIFFERENT PARTS OF THE COUNTRY

The numbers indicate the part from which the cuts are taken, as shown on the chart (Fig. No. 7).

1. Neck, part of the Rattleran, and Sticking piece.

2. Chuck, part of Rattleran.

3. Chuck and Rib roasts.

4. Sirloin steak, Porter-house steak, Pinbone roast. The latter includes also a part of Number 7.

5. Rump, Aitchbone.

6. Round.

7. Flank, Top of Sirloin.

8. Flank, Plate.

9. Brisket, Navel.

10. Shoulder, Shoulder clod, Rattleran, Bolar, Cross ribs.

11. and 12. Fore and hind shin, Soup bones.

13. Vein, Veiny piece.

Care of meat. All meat should at once be removed from the wrapping paper when it comes from the store, otherwise the paper absorbs the juices and sticks to the meat. Never put meat into water, except it be such parts as kidney, liver, heart, etc., or the water will soak out the juice which is the part of meat that contains the flavour. Wipe it with a clean, wet cloth, and keep it in a cool place. If it must be kept longer than is safe for raw meat, it may be partially cooked, cooled quickly, and kept cold till time to complete the cooking.

Cooking meat. If meat is put into cold water and gradually heated to the boiling point, a large proportion of the juice will be extracted. The meat will thus be rendered tasteless and the water will contain the flavouring matter. Long cooking in water dissolves the gelatine of the bones and connective tissue. These effects are desirable for soups and broths, but undesirable when the meat itself is also to be used.

If meat is put into boiling water, allowed to boil a few minutes, and then cooked a long time at a lower temperature, the albumen of the juice is hardened on the surface of the meat and the remaining juice is thus kept to a considerable extent. The long cooking may then soften the tough tissue while the meat retains much of its flavour, the water becoming also flavoured. This is desirable for stews, meat pies, pot roasts, poultry, etc., in which cases meat and liquor are both to be served.

Braised Beef

Wipe the beef with a wet cloth, cut off any tough ends and bone if it will not mar the appearance of the meat, as these parts will not become palatable in the length of time required for the remainder of the roast. They will be found useful for soups, stews, cannelon of beef, Hamburg steak, and such dishes. Roast the meat in a hot oven for half an hour, transfer it quickly to a cooker utensil, add enough boiling water to nearly cover it, let the whole become very hot in the oven, and place it quickly in the cooker. The time that is required for completing the cooking will depend upon the size of the piece and the degree of cooking desired. A five-pound roast may be cooked four hours, and if not found done to taste, it can be reheated to boiling point and cooked longer. A larger roast will require more time in the cooker. If preferred, the meat may first be partially cooked in the hay-box and browned in the oven afterward. It must then be boiled for half an hour, cooked three or more hours in the cooker, and then roasted. Lay a piece of raw fat on top of the roast, or baste it with drippings to assist in the browning.

Pot Roast

3 lbs. beef rump
3 cups boiling water
1 bay leaf
1 small onion
Salt and pepper
2 small carrots
2 sprigs parsley
1/2 teaspoon celery seed, or
1/4 cup celery, cut in pieces
Flour
1/2 teaspoon Worcestershire sauce

Have the butcher bone and roll the meat, dredge it well with salt, pepper, and flour, and brown it on all sides in a frying-pan with a little of the fat from the meat, or one or two tablespoons of beef drippings or pork fat. Put all the ingredients together in a small cooker-pail, let it simmer thirty minutes, set it into a larger pail of boiling water and put into a cooker for nine hours or more. Reheat it to boiling point; strain and thicken the liquor for gravy. Roundof beef may be used for pot roast, but it is drier than the rump, which has some fat on it. Four or five pounds of rump will make three pounds when boned. Have the bone sent from the market to use for soup stock.

Serves ten or twelve persons.

Beef à la Mode

3 lbs. beef from the round
1 oz. fat, salt pork
2 teaspoons salt
1/4 teaspoon pepper
Flour
1 onion
1/8 teaspoon allspice
1/8 teaspoon nutmeg
6 cloves
2 tablespoons rendered beef fat
Water to nearly cover it

Wash the meat, lard it with the pork cut into strips, or gash it deeply and insert the pork in the gashes. Dredge it with the salt, pepper, and flour, and fry it in the beef fat till well browned on all sides. Put the meat and other ingredients into a two or three quart cooker-pail or pan, and nearly cover the meat with boiling water. Let it simmer for half an hour, then stand the pail in a larger cooker-pail of boiling water and put it into a cooker for from nine to twelve hours. Unless several times this recipe is cooked at once, do not allow the meat to cook more than twelve hours, or it may ferment. Reheat it before serving. Strain and thicken the gravy.

Serves ten or twelve persons.

Corned Beef

Order eight or ten pounds of rump of beef corned for four days. Put it into a large cooker-pail and fill the pail with cold water. When it boils, allow it to simmer for thirty or forty minutes, then put it into a hay-box for ten or twelve hours. Reheat it before serving it. If ordinary corned beef is used it will be more delicate if, when it is allowed to come to a boil, the water is changed and fresh boiling water added. It may then be cooked as directed above for that specially corned.

Serves twenty or twenty-five persons.

Boiled Dinner

2 lbs. lean, salt pork
3 turnips
4 beets
2 carrots
1 head cabbage
12 potatoes
½ teaspoon pepper
Water to cover

Wash the pork and gash it in slices; wash and pare the vegetables. If preferred, the beets may be cooked separately, without paring them. Put all, except the potatoes, into the cooker-pail and cover them with boiling water. When boiling let them cook ten minutes on the stove, then put the pail into the cooker for six hours or more. Add the potatoes, reheat it to boiling point, and replace it in the cooker for two hours. If more salt or pepper is required add it when the potatoes are put in. In order to save time the potatoes may be cooked separately, drained and added to the dinner before bringing it to a boil for serving. Corned beef may be used in place of pork, if preferred.

Serves eight or ten persons.

59

Beef Stew à la Mode

1½ lbs. beef brisket
Flour
4 tablespoons rendered fat
1 onion
⅛ teaspoon pepper
6 cloves
2 teaspoons salt
2 slices lemon
⅛ teaspoon ground allspice
⅛ teaspoon nutmeg
Water to cover (about 1 pt.)

Buy two and one-half or three pounds of brisket to get one and one-half pounds of clear, lean meat. Cut the meat into one inch pieces, roll them in flour, and fry them in the fat till brown. The onion may be sliced and added when the meat is nearly brown. Put the meat with the other ingredients into a small cooker-pail, cover it with hot water, boil for ten minutes, and cook it in a hay-box for five hours or more. If left for many hours the meat becomes a trifle dry, but otherwise the stew is not injured by overcooking. The gravy may be thickened, if desired, with flour and water mixed together in equal parts. The bones may be put in with the stew during the cooking and removed before serving, or they may be used to make soup stock.

Serves five or six persons.

Stuffed Rolled Steak

1 flank steak
1 cup soft breadcrumbs
1 teaspoon salt
⅛ teaspoon pepper
2 tablespoons butter
½ teaspoon thyme or summer savoury
1 tablespoon chopped parsley

Wash the steak and remove the membrane that covers it, unless that has been done at the market. Make a stuffing of the crumbs, melting the butter and adding the crumbs and other ingredients to it. If the steak is large enough, use more stuffing than one cupful. Spread the stuffing over the meat to within two inches of the edge. Roll and skewer or tie it into shape. Brown it well on all sides in a dry frying-pan, or dredge it with flour and fry it in rendered beef fat. Lay it in a small cooker-pail or pan. Make two cupfuls of Brown Sauce, or enough to cover the roll. Boil the roll for two minutes and set the pail in a larger pail of boiling water. Put it for five or six hours into a cooker. When it is to be served, remove the string or skewers, lay the roll on a platter, and pour the gravy over it.

Round steak, cut about one-half inch thick, may be used. Remove the bone before rolling it.

Beef Stew with Dumplings

2 cups cooked or raw beef
2 cups raw or cooked potatoes
2/3 cup tomato
1 onion, cut in slices
4 tablespoons rendered fat or butter
1 teaspoon salt
1/8 teaspoon pepper
1/3 cup flour
1 tablespoon chopped parsley
1 1/2 cups water, or more

If cooked meat and potatoes are used, cut them in three-quarter-inch dice, make a brown sauce of the fat, flour, seasoning, and water, add the vegetables and meat and enough water to just cover the stew. Place the dumplings on top, boil it for five minutes, and cook in a hay-box for one and one-quarter hours. If the meat is tough it will be better to treat it like raw beef. If raw beef is used, cut it in pieces, bring it to a boil with the water, and put it into the cooker for three or four hours before adding the other ingredients.

Dumplings for Stew

2 cups flour
2 tablespoons lard or butter
4 teaspoons baking powder
1/2 teaspoon salt
3/4 to 1 cup water

Sift the flour, salt, and baking powder together, work the fat into them with the fingers, or cut it in with a knife. Add enough water to make a stiff dough. Drop it by tablespoonfuls on the top of the stew. The dumplings should rest on the meat and vegetables, as they will not be so light if submerged in the gravy.

Serves six or seven persons.

Irish Stew

    3 cups meat
    2 cups potatoes
    1/2 cup turnip
    1/2 cup carrot
    1/3 cup onion
    1/2 cup celery
    2 teaspoons salt
    1/4 teaspoon pepper
    1/3 cup flour
    4 tablespoons rendered fat
    3 cups water

Wash and cut about two pounds of beef, from the leg, brisket or other cheap cuts, into one-inch pieces. Remove most of the fat, or all of it, if desired. Wash and pare the turnip and carrot and cut them into small pieces. Pare the potatoes and cut them into one-inch cubes. Slice the onion and cut the celery into small pieces. Roll the meat in the flour and fry it till it is brown in the fat. Put all the ingredients, except the remaining flour, into a cooker-pail and, when boiling, put them into a cooker for five hours. Mix the remaining flour with an equal quantity of cold water. Stir it into the stew, and when it has boiled it is ready to serve. It will not be harmed by being kept hot in the cooker for another hour or more.

Serves eight or ten persons.

Cannelon of Beef

    1 lb. lean beef, chopped
    Grated rind 1/4 lemon
    1 tablespoon chopped parsley
    1 cup soft breadcrumbs
    1 teaspoon scraped onion
    2 tablespoons butter or rendered fat beef
    1/8 tablespoon nutmeg
    1/2 tablespoon salt
    1/8 teaspoon pepper
    2 eggs

Mix in the order given, add the eggs, which have been slightly beaten, put it into a well-greased one-quart brown bread mould or water-tight can. Stand the mould in a large pail of water, arranged on a rack, if necessary to raise the top of the mould to the level of the top of the pail. Fill the pail with boiling water, to within one-third of the top of the mould. Boil it for one-half hour and put it into a cooker for four hours. If several times this recipe is used, and put into larger moulds, it should be boiled a longer time. It is good served hot, with brown sauce, or cold.

Serves six or eight persons.

Meat Pie

> 2 cups cooked or raw meat
> 2 cups potatoes
> 1 cup tomatoes
> 2 sprigs parsley, chopped
> 1/2 teaspoon celery salt
> 2 onions
> 1 teaspoon salt
> 1/4 teaspoon pepper
> 1/4 cup flour
> 1 bay leaf, broken fine
> Water (about 1 pt.)

If cooked meat is used, cut it into three-quarter-inch cubes. Cut the potatoes into similar pieces, slice the onions, put all the ingredients, but the flour, together in a cooker-pail or pan, add the boiling water, and, when boiling, add the flour mixed to a paste with an equal quantity of water. Boil five minutes and put it into a cooker for two hours or more. Raw meat will require five hours or more. If the stewed mixture is not in a pan suitable for baking, transfer it to a baking-pan or dish, cover with a crust and bake for one-half hour.

Crust for Meat Pie

> 1 1/2 cups flour
> 3 teaspoons baking powder
> 1/3 teaspoon salt
> 1 1/2 tablespoons butter
> 1/2 cup water, or more

Mix and sift the dry ingredients, work in the fat, and put in enough water to make a dough stiff enough to roll on a board. Roll it out to the dish and bake it. An inverted cup in the centre of the pie, under the crust, will prevent the gravy from boiling over during the baking.

Serves six or eight persons.

Braised Beef's Liver

    1 liver
    1/4 lb. fat salt pork
    1 onion
    Flour
    Fat
    2 teaspoons sage leaves
    2 teaspoons thyme
    1 teaspoon salt
    1/4 teaspoon pepper
    Water to cover

Lard the liver with the pork. Dredge it with flour and brown it in a frying-pan, with rendered beef or pork fat or butter. Put it into a cooker-pail or pan just large enough to hold it. Cover it with boiling water, boil it for five minutes, set the pail in a larger cooker-pail of boiling water, and put it into a cooker for ten hours or more. Reheat it and serve it on a platter, cutting it through, but not separating the slices. Pour over it the gravy, which has been strained and thickened with flour and water mixed to a paste.

The number of persons that it will serve depends upon the size of the liver. Allow one pound for three or four persons.

Beef Kidney

Wash and soak two kidneys in a large amount of water, for several hours or over night, changing the water at least once. Cut them open, rinse them and put them on to boil in boiling salted water to barely cover them, in a small cooker-pail. Let them boil five minutes, set the pail in a larger pail of boiling water, and cook them ten hours or more in a cooker. When tender, remove the tubes and membranes and slice the kidneys. Thicken as much of the gravy as you wish to use, with one-fourth of a cupful of flour mixed with one-fourth of a cupful of water to each pint ofgravy. Add the sliced kidneys and serve them when they are boiling hot.

Stuffed Heart

1 heart
½ cup crumbs
1 tablespoon butter
½ teaspoon salt
⅛ teaspoon pepper
1 small onion, chopped
½ teaspoon powdered thyme
1 thick slice bacon
Flour

Wash the heart, remove the arteries and veins and squeeze out any clots of blood that there may be. Stuff it with the soft bread crumbs to which the seasonings and melted butter have been added. Try out the fat from the slice of bacon, dredge the heart with salt, pepper and flour and brown it on all sides in the bacon fat. Put the heart and the crisp bacon into as small a cooker-pail as will hold it, cover it with boiling water, boil it for five minutes and put the pail into a larger cooker-pail with as much boiling water as it will hold when the small pail is in place. Put it into a cooker for ten hours, or over night. Boil it again and cook it for three or four hours. Reheat it when ready to serve it, thickening each pint of the gravy with one-fourth cup of flour and an equal quantity of water mixed to a smooth paste. The heart will look more attractive if sliced and covered with gravy before serving.

Beef or calf's heart may be cooked without a stuffing and served with caper sauce.

Corned Tongue

Wash the tongue, put it into a cooker-pail of from four to six quarts capacity. Fill the pail with cold water, bring the tongue to a boil and boil it for from twenty minutes to half an hour, depending upon its size. Put it into a cooker for ten or twelve hours. If not perfectly tender, bring it again to a boil and cook it from two to four hours longer. Plunge it into cold water, remove the skin, and serve it cold, cut in thin slices.

Fresh Tongue

1 tongue
1 onion
1 bay leaf

1 teaspoon peppercorns
8 cloves
Salt

Wash the tongue, put it into as small a cooker-pail as will easily hold it, add the other ingredients and fill the pail with boiling water, using one teaspoonful of salt to each quart of water. Let it boil for twenty minutes or half an hour, depending upon the size of the tongue. Put it into a cooker for ten hours or more. If not perfectly tender, reheat it to boiling point and cook it for from two to four hours longer in the hay-box. Plunge it into cold water and remove the skin. Serve it hot with caper sauce, using the liquor in which the tongue was boiled in place of water, to make the sauce.

XIII

LAMB AND MUTTON

Spring lamb is the meat of lambs from six weeks to three months old. It is obtainable in March and throughout the spring. Yearling is lamb one year old. The flesh of lamb is lighter in colour than that of mutton and the bones are pinker. It may be distinguished from mutton, also, by the smaller size of the cuts, which are otherwise the same in mutton and lamb. Mutton, as all dark meats, may be served rare; but lamb, being lighter, is classed with white meats in this respect, and should be thoroughly cooked. The rank flavour of mutton is greatly reduced if the pink membrane, which surrounds the animal, is pulled off before cooking. The fat of mutton has a strong, disagreeable flavour, and most of it should be removed. It will not be good for any cooking purposes as veal, beef, and pork fat are.

Cuts of Mutton. The favourite cuts are the rib and loin chops and the leg, but as other parts of the sheep are much cheaper, it is well to know their possibilities. Shoulder, boned and tied intoshape, will, when cooked in the hay-box or cooker, make a very good substitute for the leg, while shoulder of lamb makes a good roast for small families who grow tired of perpetual steak and chops.

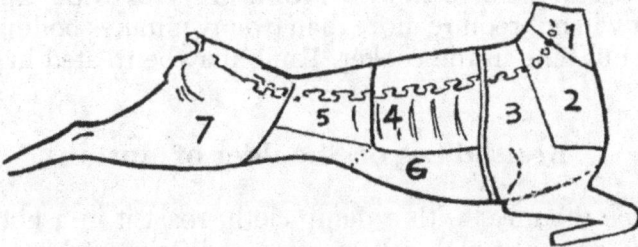

Figure No. 8
Diagram of the cuts of mutton and lamb.

TABLE SHOWING THE WAYS IN WHICH THE VARIOUS CUTS OF MUTTON AND LAMB MAY BE COOKED IN THE HAY-BOX OR COOKER

1. Neck, stews and broth.
2. Chuck, stews, broth, meat pie, casserole of rice and meat, hash.

67

3. Shoulder, braising, plain or boned and stuffed, casserole of rice and meat, hash.

4 and 5. Loin chops, cooked as veal cutlets, breaded or plain.

6. Flank, soups, stews.

7. Leg, braised or boiled.

OTHER PARTS OF THE ANIMAL, USED FOR FOOD, WHICH MAY BE COOKED IN THE HAY-BOX OR COOKER

Heart, braised, plain or stuffed.
Liver, braised, or breaded as veal cutlets.
Tongue, boiled.
Kidneys, stewed.

In the chapter on the Insulated Oven directions are also given for roasting some cuts of mutton and lamb. They are not included in this list, since the oven is not an accompaniment of every cooker.

Boiled Leg or Shoulder of Mutton

Wipe the meat with a damp cloth, put it into a cooker-pail with boiling salted water enough to cover it, and to permit of at least three or four quarts of water being used, the amount depending upon the size of the leg. Boil it for half an hour and cook it in the cooker for six hours or more. The broth should be saved for soup stock and gravy. Serve it with brown gravy or with caper sauce. Shoulder will not require more than twenty minutes boiling, but will take the full time in the cooker. Lamb may be treated in the same manner.

Braised Leg or Shoulder of Mutton

Wipe the meat with a damp cloth, roast it in a hot oven till brown, or dredge it with salt, pepper, and flour, and brown it in a frying-pan; put it, while still hot, into a cooker-pail with enough boiling water to half cover it, or more. Bring it to a hard boil, while tightly covered, put it at once into a cooker for six hours or more. Serve it with brown gravy, saving the remaining broth for soup stock. Lamb may be treated in the same manner.

Mutton Stew

2 cups meat
2/3 cup tomato

68

1 onion
1 tablespoon chopped parsley
2 cups potatoes
1 teaspoon salt
1/8 teaspoon pepper
1 1/2 cups water, or more
1/4 cup butter, lard or beef fat
1/3 cup flour

Wipe the meat with a damp cloth, cut it into three-quarter-inch cubes, put it into a cooker-pail with all the other ingredients, except the fat and flour. The potatoes should be pared and cut into one and one-half-inch cubes. Bring all to a boil, boil it for five minutes and put it into a cooker for from four to six hours. Make a brown sauce, using the fat, flour, and liquor from the stew. Heat the stew in this till boiling. Or the meat may be dredged with the flour and fried in the fat until meat and flour are brown, before being put into the cooker. If cooked meat is used, one and one-half hours in the cooker will be enough, unless the meat is very tough, in which case it may be cooked as long as raw meat. The addition of one green pepper makes a good variation of this stew.

Serves five or six persons.

Chestnut Stew

2 cups raw mutton
2 onions
2 tablespoons fat
3 tablespoons flour
3 cups blanched nuts
2 teaspoons salt
1/4 teaspoon pepper
Water

Wipe the meat with a damp cloth, cut it into three-quarter-inch cubes; peel and slice the onions. Dredge the meat with the flour, brown it and the onions in a frying-pan with any fat suitable for cooking. Put all the ingredients into a cooker-pail, barely cover them with boiling water, and let the stew boil five minutes before putting it into a cooker for four hours or more.

Serves six or eight persons.

Syrian Stew (Yakhni)
2 cups raw mutton

2 tablespoons fat
3 tablespoons flour
2 cups string beans
2 onions
2 cups tomatoes
1½ teaspoons salt
⅙ teaspoon pepper
Water

Wipe the meat with a damp cloth, cut it into cubes, dredge it with the flour, and brown it in the fat. Put all the ingredients together, scraping from the frying-pan all of the flour and fat. Add enough water to barely cover them, let them boil for five minutes, and put them into the cooker for six hours or more, depending upon the beans. If they are old and tough they may require more than six hours to cook.

In Syria this stew is always served with boiled or steamed rice. Serves six or eight persons.

Okra Stew

2 cups raw mutton
2 tablespoons fat
⅛ cup flour
2 onions
2 cups tomatoes
2 cups okra
1½ teaspoons salt
⅙ teaspoon pepper
Water

Wipe the meat with a damp cloth, cut it into cubes. Wash and cut the okra in pieces, dredge it and the meat with the flour and fry them, till brown, in the fat. Put all the ingredients into a cooker-pail, add enough water to barely cover them, boil them for five minutes, and put them into a cooker for four hours, or more.

Serves six or eight persons.

Syrian Stuffed Cabbage

1 cup raw chopped meat
2 tablespoons fat
⅓ cup raw rice
2 teaspoons salt

¼ teaspoon pepper
1 head cabbage
½ lemon

Strip off the leaves from a head of cabbage, throw them into boiling water, and let them stand till they are wilted. Mix the remaining ingredients, except the lemon, using for the meat either mutton or beef. Lay a cabbage leaf on a plate, remove the thickest part of the midrib, so that it will roll. Spread on it a rounded teaspoonful of the mixture and roll it like a cigarette. Do the same with the other leaves, packing each one, as it is finished, into a pan which will fit over a cooker-pail, unless a pail is used which will be nearly filled by the cabbage. The rolls must be carefully packed or they will float and unroll when the water is added. Cover them with boiling water, bring all to a boil, and boil it for five minutes, then put it directly into a cooker, if the pail is full, or over boiling water if not, and leave it for from four to six hours. Take the rolls out carefully with a cake turner or skimmer, lay them in a platter, and squeeze the juice of half a lemon over them. They are usually served as the meat dish for luncheon.

Serves six or eight persons.

Casserole of Rice and Meat

4 cups cooked rice (1 cup raw)
2 cups cooked mutton
1 teaspoon salt
¼ teaspoon pepper
1 teaspoon grated onion
1 tablespoon chopped parsley
¼ cup breadcrumbs
1 egg
Stock or water

Line a greased mould of one and one-half quarts' capacity with three cups of the rice. Remove all the fat from the meat, chop it fine, and mix it with the other ingredients, adding enough stock or water to barely keep it from crumbling. Pack the meat into the mould and cover it with the remaining cupful of rice. Grease the cover and put it on. Stand the mould in a large cooker-pail of water to two-thirds of its depth, or, if it is shallow, prop it on a rack, so that the water will reach half its depth; boil it for fifteen minutes, and cook it for one hour or more in the cooker. Turn it out carefully on to a hot platter, and pour tomato sauce around, but not over it.

Serves six or eight persons.

Ragout of Cold Mutton

2 cups cold mutton
1 onion, sliced
1 cup mutton stock
2 tablespoons butter
1/2 can peas
1 teaspoon salt
1/4 teaspoon pepper
1 head of lettuce
Farina balls

Cut the mutton into one-inch cubes. Put all the ingredients except the lettuce and farina balls into a cooker-pail together, cover it closely, and when boiling put it into a cooker for one hour. Serve it on a platter garnished with lettuce leaves and farina balls.

Serves four to six persons.

XIV

VEAL

Veal varies greatly with the age of the calf from which it is taken. It should be pink, with firm, white fat. Pale, flabby veal comes from calves which have been killed too young, or bled before death, and is likely to be tasteless and stringy when cooked. The older veal grows, the more like beef it appears. The cuts are larger and the colour is darker and more like the red of beef. Veal can be purchased the year round, but the best season for it is spring and summer. Almost all parts of the calf are tender, but the cheaper cuts correspond with the cheaper cuts of beef, except the cutletsor steaks, which are taken from the same part of the animal as the round of beef, and command a good price. Veal, like other white meats, should be thoroughly cooked. Its delicacy commends it for many purposes, but it often requires the addition of pork, or high seasoning, to give it flavour.

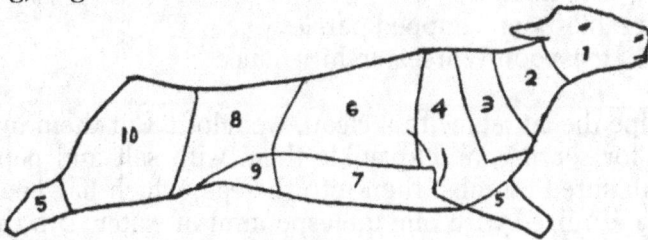

Figure No. 9
Diagram of the cuts of veal.

TABLE SHOWING THE WAYS IN WHICH THE VARIOUS CUTS OF VEAL MAY BE COOKED IN THE HAY-BOX OR COOKER

1. Head, Jelly, soups, and broths, calf's head à la terrapin.
2. Neck, Stews, soup, veal pie.
3. Chuck, Veal loaf, stews, soup, veal pie.
4. Shoulder, Braised, stuffed and braised.
5. Shanks, Soups.
6. Ribs, Braised or breaded as veal cutlets.
7. Breast, Soups, stews, veal loaf.
8. Loin, Braised or breaded as veal cutlets.
9. Flank, Soups or stews.
10. Leg, Breaded cutlets or plain cutlets.

73

OTHER PARTS OF THE CALF, USED FOR FOOD, WHICH MAY BE COOKED IN THE HAY-BOX OR COOKER

Brains, Stewed and creamed.
Heart, Braised, plain or stuffed.
Liver, Braised, or stewed.
Tongues, Boiled.
Sweetbreads, Stewed or creamed.
Kidneys, Stewed or creamed.

Breaded Veal Cutlets

2 lbs. veal cutlets
Fine, dry breadcrumbs
Salt
Pepper
1 egg
1 pt. water or stock
1/2 cup butter or drippings
1/3 cup flour
1 tablespoon chopped parsley
1/2 teaspoon Worcestershire Sauce

Wipe the cutlets with a clean, wet cloth. Cut them into pieces suitable for serving, and sprinkle them with salt and pepper. Dip them into sifted crumbs, then into the egg, which has been beaten slightly and mixed with one tablespoonful of water. Dip the cutlets again into the crumbs and fry them until they are a rich brown, in one-half the butter or drippings. Put them into a small cooker-pail or pan. Make Brown Sauce, using the remaining ingredients. Pour the sauce over the cutlets and, when boiling, stand the pail in a large cooker-pail of boiling water. Put it into a cooker for from two to four hours, depending upon the age and toughness of the veal. Reheat them before serving.

Serves six or eight persons.

Plain Veal Cutlets

Wipe the cutlets with a wet cloth, trim off any tough membranes, and cut them into pieces suitable for serving. Brown them in a very hot frying-pan with butter or rendered fat, beingcareful not to let them scorch. Sprinkle them well with salt and pepper and put them into a small cooker-pail or pan. Pour a little boiling water into the frying-pan and, when all the brown juice which has hardened on the pan has been dissolved, pour this over the cutlets. Add enough boiling water to barely cover them and, when boiling, stand the pail or pan in a large cooker-pail of boiling water. Put it into the cooker for from two to four hours, depending upon the age and toughness of the veal. Reheat them before serving, if necessary.

Veal Loaf

2 cups minced veal
2 eggs
1/4 cup melted butter
1 cup soft bread crumbs
1/8 teaspoon pepper
11/2 teaspoons salt
2 tablespoons chopped parsley
2 tablespoons chopped onion
1/4 inch slice fat salt pork
1/2 teaspoon ground sage

Wipe meat from the cheaper cuts of veal, remove the fat and toughest membranes, and put it through a fine food-chopper. Mix the seasonings with the crumbs, add the melted butter, mix these with the veal, add the pork and, lastly, the eggs. Put the mixture in a well-buttered one-quart brown bread mould or water-tight can. Spread it level but do not pack it in the mould. Stand it in a large cooker-pail with enough boiling water to come at least two-thirds of the way up the mould. Boil it for twenty minutes and put it into the cooker for four hours. Serve it either hot or cold.

Serves eight or ten persons.

Sweetbreads

Wash and soak the sweetbreads in cold water for one hour. Plunge them into boiling salted water (one teaspoonful of salt for each quart of water). Boil them two minutes and put them into the cooker for two hours. Plunge them into cold water, remove the membrane which covers them, and they are then ready to be broken in pieces for creamed sweetbreads or rolled in crumbs and egg and fried.

Creamed Sweetbreads

Make a white sauce, using part milk and part cream, if

desired. To each cupful of sauce add two cupfuls of prepared sweetbreads broken into small pieces, let them come to a boil and serve them at once, or put them into a cooker to keep warm until they are needed.

Calf's Heart

Calf's heart may be cooked as beef's heart, except that it will not require so long to cook. Ten minutes is sufficient to allow for cooking over the flame, and ten hours in the hay-box.

Calf's Liver

Prepare and cook it in the same manner as beef's liver, allowing only four hours for it to cook in the hay-box.

Veal Kidney

These are almost as delicate as sweetbreads. They may be cooked for two hours in the same manner as beef kidney, or creamed or fried as sweetbreads.

Calf's Head à la Terrapin

1 calf's head
Salt
Water
2 tablespoons butter
2 tablespoons flour
1/8 teaspoon pepper
1/2 cup cream
4 egg yolks
Madeira Wine

Carefully clean a calf's head and put it into a cooker-pail. Cover it with boiling water, add one teaspoonful of salt to each quart of water and let it boil for twenty minutes. Put it into a cooker for nine hours or more. Cool it and cut the face meat into small dice. Make a cupful of sauce using the butter, flour, pepper, one-half teaspoonful of salt and one cupful of the water in which the head was boiled. Add the cream and, when boiling, the raw yolks of two eggs which have been slightly beaten. Stir it constantly for about two minutes until the eggs have cooked. Then add two tablespoonfuls of Madeira wine and the yolks of two hard-cooked eggs cut into quarters.

Serves five or six persons.

XV

PORK

Whatever may be true of the extent to which pork and pork products are wholesome for particular individuals, there can be no doubt that its delicious flavour will insure its being eaten by a large number of people who either do not know or do not care whether it agrees with them or not. Experiments undertaken under the management of the Department of Agriculture[1] have resulted in the conclusion that pork is as thoroughly and easily digested, under normal conditions of health, as any meat, although personal experience would indicate that pork does not agree with some people as well as other kinds of meat. It is specially important, however, that pork be very well cooked or well cured, in order to insure against the danger from trichinosis. We are told by B. H. Ransom[2] that it is only by eating raw or insufficiently cooked or cured pork that there is thought to be any danger of this disease. Curing is the process of smoking, salting, or combined salting and smoking of meat, which acts as a preservative for it. We thus see that, not only because it is a white meat, as mentioned in the chapter on veal, pork and pork products should be cooked until very well done.

As pork is the fattest of all meats, it is suitable for a cold-weather diet and will probably be found to agree better at that season. For whatever reason it may be, fresh pork seems to be less wholesome than when cured, bacon having the reputation of being one of the most easily digested of all fats.

Young pigs (four weeks old) are frequently dressed and roasted whole.

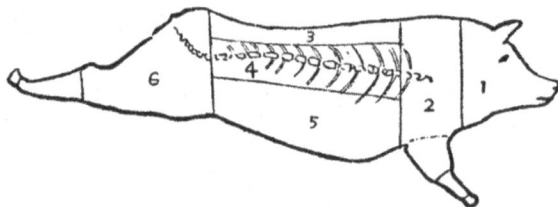

Figure No. 10
Diagram of the cuts of pork.

---

[1] Office of Experiment Stations, Bulletin 193, 1907
[2] U. S. Dept. of Agriculture, Bureau of Animal Industry, Circular 108, 1907

Pork is usually cut for market in the manner illustrated in figure No. 10.

The back is fat and is used for salt pork or lard. The ribs are used for spare-ribs, and the loin or chine, which is the backbone with its adhering meat, is used for roasts or chops. The legs are roasted, if fresh, or they are cured, by salting and smoking, for hams, sugar being used in the salting process, which gives the name "sugar-cured hams"; the shoulders are treated in the same way and may be used very much as hams, although the flesh is not so thick and the proportion of bone is greater. The belly is cured for bacon, the head and feet are soused or pickled, and the trimmings of fat and lean are chopped, highly seasoned, and used for sausage, or combined with meal and made into scrapple.

To select fresh pork. The meat should be firm and of a pale red colour, the fat hard and white and the skin white and clear. Yellowish fat, with kernels in it, and soft, flabby flesh are an indication of inferior pork.

Boiled Ham or Shoulder

Put a ham or shoulder in a large enough cooker-pail to allow of its being covered with eight or ten quarts of water. A special oblong or extra deep utensil may be required for cooking hams and such very large cuts of meat. Put in the ham, add cold water to fill the utensil, and bring it to a boil. This will serve to draw out a good deal of the salt from the meat and will not extract much of the meat flavour, if the ham be whole. A cut ham may be covered with boiling water which will seal the pores on the surface of the meat and help to retain its juices. Allow the ham to simmer for twenty minutes, or, if very large, for one-half hour, then put it into a cooker for seven hours or more. The larger the ham the greater the quantity of water must be, a fifteen-pound ham taking as much as fifteen quarts of water. Success in cooking large cuts of meat will depend to a great extent upon using sufficient water.

Fresh Pork with Sauerkraut

Wash and gash a two-pound piece of fresh, lean pork into slices. Put it with one quart of sauerkraut into a cooker-pail of boiling salted water. Let it boil for fifteen minutes, tightly covered. Place it in a cooker for eight or ten hours. Reheat till boiling, drain it, and serve the pork in a platter, with the sauerkraut arranged as a border; or put the sauerkraut into a vegetable dish. It grows cold quickly and must be served promptly and on hot dishes.

Serves six or eight persons.

Head Cheese

Cut a hog's head into four pieces. Remove the brain, ears, skin, snout, and eyes. Cut off the fat to try out for lard. Put the lean and bony parts to soak in cold water over night to extract the blood. Clean the head thoroughly, put it into a cooker-pail, cover it with cold water, boil it for fifteen minutes and put it into the cooker for ten hours or more. If the meat will not then slip readily from the bones, bring it again to a boil and put it into the cooker until it will (perhaps six hours more). Remove the bones and hard gristle, drain off the liquor, reserving it for future use. Put the meat through a food-chopper, return it to the cooker-pail with enough of the liquor to cover it, and salt, pepper, and powdered sage to taste. Let it boil, put it into a cooker for an hour or more, then pour it into a shallow pan or dish; cover it with cheese-cloth and a board with a weight, to hold it in place. When cold it will be solid, and is ready to serve, thinly sliced.

Souse

Treat a hog's head in the same manner as for head cheese, adding a little vinegar with the other seasonings.

Scrapple

Treat a hog's head in the same manner as for head cheese, up to the point where the liquor is added to the chopped meat. The heart and liver may also be cooked with the head, and any scraps or bloody parts of the meat may be soaked and cooked with it. When the meat is freed from bone, gristle, and skin, and chopped finely, and all the liquor is added to it, it is seasoned with salt, pepper, sage, thyme or marjoram, and brought to a boil. Enough corn-meal, or corn-meal and buckwheat flour in the proportion of one-third cupful of buckwheat to two-thirds of a cupful of corn-meal, is added, to make the mixture of the consistency of corn-meal mush. About one cupful of the two combined will be required for each three pints of the pork mixture. Let this come to a boil, stirring it constantly; boil it five minutes, and put it into a cooker for four hours or more. Pour it into a mould or bread pan and, when cold, slice and fry it like sausage.

80

Pickled Pigs' Feet

Wash the pigs' feet, soak them in warm water for one-half hour, then scrub and scrape them well; soak them again for twelve hours in cold, salted water, and clean them again. If necessary, singe them; remove the toes, and bring them to a boil in salted water to more than cover them. Boil them five minutes, and cook them for ten hours or more in a cooker. If not tender, reheat them till boiling, and cook them again. Remove them from the water, split them with a cleaver, unless this is done before cooking, pack them in a jar, and cover them with hot, spiced vinegar, preferably made from white wine. They are eaten cold, or dipped in batter and fried.

XVI

POULTRY

In buying poultry select that which has clean, unbroken skin and is as fat as possible. Young chickens have often a darker appearance than old, owing to the fact that there is less fat under the skin or that the skin is thinner. They have few hairs, many pin-feathers, and the end of the breast-bone, toward the tail, is limber and cartilaginous. In old chickens (fowl) this bone is stiff, there are many hairs, few pin-feathers, and the scales on the legs are hard and horny. The wing joint is firm in old chickens, but is sometimes broken by poultry dealers in order to make the purchaser think the poultry younger than it is.

Chickens are frequently kept in cold storage for months, or even years, and they undergo decided changes during these periods. The effect of eating such storage poultry is still under debate; but, while there is uncertainty as to whether they may not be responsible for some obscure intestinal disorders or other disturbances, it is well to know how to tell them from fresh-killed birds. In an article entitled "Changes Taking Place in Chickens in Cold Storage," in the Yearbook of the Department of Agriculture, for 1907, we read that the fresh chicken is a pale, soft yellow, without any tinge or suggestion of green in the colour of the skin, while there is enough translucency to show through it the delicate pink of the muscles underneath. It can be plainly seen that the pink tint is not of the skin itself. While the skin is perfectly flexible, and is not adherent over any part of the body, it is well filled by the tissues below, so that areas distended by either fluids or gases are wanting. The feather papillæ are perfectly distinct, and, though of the same tint as the skin, are plainly visible because of their elevation. In those regions where the papillæ are most numerous, or support heavier feathers, they lend a much brighter yellow hue to the skin. The neck is smooth and well rounded, the comb and gills red, and the eye full.

With storage birds the skin becomes somewhat dried, and finally quite leathery and stretched in appearance; is less translucent than that of the fresh, and the feather papillæ tend to flatten and disappear. In time the colour of the skin alters in places to browns, reds, purples, or greenish tints.

Care of poultry. Poultry should be drawn as soon as purchased, if it has not been already done; it should be wiped out with a dry cloth, if not to be cooked immediately, and kept in a cold place. Old chickens can be made as tender as young chickens in a cooker, and will have more flavour.

To draw poultry. Cut off the head, turn back the skin of the neck and cut off the neck close to the body. If the crop has food in it, remove it from the neck, otherwise it will come out with the other organs. Cut off the windpipe. Make an opening above the vent with a small sharp knife, cut around the vent, being careful not to cut into the intestine. Put the hand just inside the wall of the body and work it carefully over the whole inner surface of the body, detaching the organs in one mass. When the hand can pass freely all around them, draw them all out together. The lungs and kidneys, imbedded in the bones, will remain behind and must be removed separately. Cut out the little oil bag on the back of the tail. Singe the chicken, and wash it well inside and outside. The heart, liver, and gizzard are the giblets, and are boiled and often used in the gravy.

To cut up a chicken. After it is drawn, a chicken may be cut for stew or fricassee, into thirteen pieces. First remove the neck, then the legs, by cutting the skin, etc., that holds them to the body; then cut on either side down to the joint which lies almost at the back. Bend the leg out from the body and this will break the ligaments that hold it. Separate the two joints of the leg in large chickens. Remove the wings by cutting around the joints and bending them out as the leg was done. Next cut off the wishbone by placing the knife across the breast and cutting close to the end of the breast-bone toward the neck. If desired, remove the meat from the breast in two fillets, beginning to cut at the top and following the bone closely, separating the meat from the breast-bone and sides of the chicken. Next cut from the back to the front, through the ribs. Separate the "side bone" from one side, and break the back in two where the ribs end.

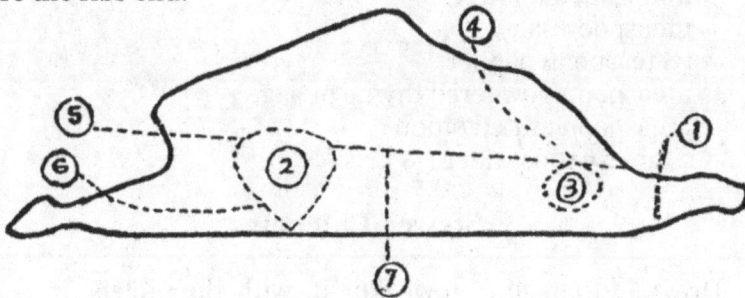

Figure No. 11.
Method of cutting chicken for stew or fricassee.

To truss poultry. Stuff the poultry two-thirdsfull, from the tail

83

opening. It may be skewered into shape, but the quickest and easiest way is to tie it. The slight mark left by the string on the breast may be covered with a garnish of parsley or fine celery leaves. Fold the neck skin under the body, putting the loop end of a doubled piece of string under it; bring the ends of string up and cross them over the breast so as to hold the wings in place; carry the string down over the thighs to the under side of the tail to hold the thighs in place, and bring it up around the tail and the ends of the drumsticks, and tie it securely. This will hold the leg bones down to the tail. If this is not sufficient to hold in the stuffing, close the opening with a skewer, or sew it with heavy thread before trussing the bird. Old chickens, turkeys, and tough ducks or geese can be stuffed, trussed, and cooked for some hours in a cooker, then be removed and browned in an oven.

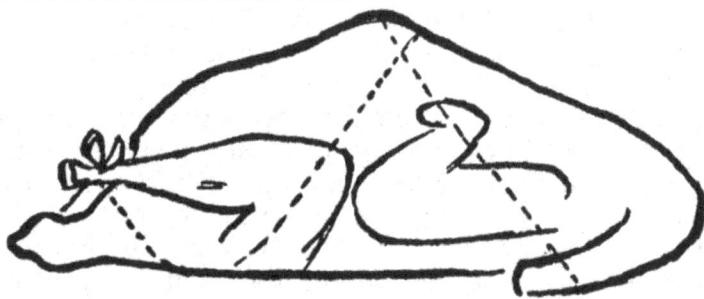

Figure No. 12
Chicken, trussed for roasting or braising.

Stuffing for Poultry

1 cup soft breadcrumbs
1 tablespoon butter
1 teaspoon salt
1/8 teaspoon pepper
1 teaspoon powdered thyme or sage
1 teaspoon grated onion
2 tablespoons water

Stewed Chicken

Draw and cut up a fowl. Put it, with the giblets, in enough boiling salted water (one teaspoonful of salt to each quart of water) to cover it. Let it boil for ten minutes and put it into a cooker for ten hours or more. If not quite tender, bring it again to a boil and cook it for from six to eight hours, depending upon its toughness. Skim off as much as possible of the fat from the liquor, pour off some of the liquor and save it to use as soup or stock, and thicken the remainder with two tablespoonfuls of flour for each cup of liquid, mixed to a paste with an equal quantity of water. A beaten egg or two, stirred into the gravy just before serving, improves it. Add pepper and salt to taste, and serve the chicken on a hot platter with the gravy poured around it. The platter may be garnished with boiled rice piled about the chicken.

Chicken Fricassee

Draw a fowl and cut it in pieces, cook it as directed for stewed chicken, dredge the cooked pieces with salt and pepper, roll them in flour and sauté them in fat taken from the stewed chicken. When richly browned, place the pieces on a hot platter and pour around them a brown sauce, made with the fat and the stock from the stewed chicken. Chicken fricassee is often served on a platter of hot toast.

Chicken Pie

Prepare and cook the chicken as for stewed chicken; cut the meat from the bones, put it into a baking-dish, cover it with chicken gravy, and put over the top a crust made as directed for meat pie on page 33. Bake this for thirty minutes in a moderate oven.

Curried Chicken

Prepare and cook one fowl as for stewed chicken, adding two onions, pared and cut into slices. Add one tablespoonful of curry powder to the flour when thickening the gravy. Or the chicken may be rolled in flour and browned in butter, and the curry powder added before putting it into the cooker. It is served with a border of boiled rice.

Creamed Chicken

Prepare and cook a fowl as directed for stewed chicken. Make White Sauce, using half chicken stock and half cream for the liquid. A little grated onion and one-fourth can of mushrooms may be added.

Braised Chicken

Draw, stuff, truss and roast a young chicken in a hot oven

until it is brown; put it into a hot cooker-pail with water about one inch deep in the pan. Cover it quickly, bring it to a boil, and put it into a cooker for two and one-half hours or more. Make a brown sauce of the liquor in the pan. The giblets may be added when the chicken is put into the water, and may be chopped and added to the gravy. Only young, tender chicken can be treated in this way. A tough bird may be trussed and cooked in water to half cover it for ten or twelve hours before it is stuffed and browned. Baste it when in the oven with fat taken from the broth.

Jellied Chicken

Draw, clean, and cut up a fowl of about four or five pounds. Put it into a cooker-pail, add one teaspoonful of salt, two or three slices of onion, and cover the fowl with boiling water. Boil it for ten minutes, then put it in the cooker for ten or twelve hours. Boil it up again and replace it in the cooker for six hours or more. Repeat this if the meat is not found to be tender enough to fall readily from the bones. Remove the meat from the bones; take off the skin and season the meat with salt and pepper. Skim off all possible fat from the liquor and boil it down to about one cupful; strain it, and take off the remaining fat. Decorate the bottom of a mould or bread pan with parsley and slices of hard-cooked egg, pack in the meat and pour over it the stock. Place the meat under a weight, and leave it in a cold place till firm.

Braised Duck

Prepare and cook the duck in the same manner as braised chicken. If the duck is tough it may be cooked for eight or more hours in water in the cooker, then stuffed and browned in the oven, basting it with fat from the broth.

Braised Goose

Prepare it as braised chicken; or, if it is tough, cook it in water in a cooker as old braised chicken, until it is nearly tender. Remove it, stuff it, and brown it in a hot oven, basting it with fat from the broth.

Potted Pigeons

Clean, stuff, and truss six pigeons, place them upright in a cooker-pail and pour over them one quart of water in which celery has been cooked. If the water was not salted for the celery, add one teaspoonful of salt. Cover the pail, boil the birds for five minutes, and put them into a cooker for five or six hours, or till tender. Remove them from the water, sprinkle them with salt and pepper, dredge them with flour, and brown the entire surface in pork fat. Make two cups of Brown Sauce, using butter and stock from the pigeons; heat the birds in this, place each one on a piece of dry toast, and pour the gravy over it. Garnish it with parsley.

XVII

VEGETABLES

GENERAL DIRECTIONS FOR COOKING VEGETABLES

The flavour of vegetables is best preserved if they are put on to cook in boiling water. For cooking in a fireless cooker the water must be salted when the vegetables are started. The expression "salted water," as used in this book, means water to each quart of which one teaspoonful of salt has been added. Such vegetables as asparagus, peas, lima beans, etc., which have a delicate flavour, must be cooked with very little water; usually in a smaller pail or pan set into a larger cooker-pail of water. All vegetables should be washed before cooking, and such as potatoes, beets, turnips, etc., should be scrubbed with a small scrubbing-brush, kept for that purpose. Few vegetables are injured by overcooking in a fireless cooker.

Asparagus

Wash, and if desired, break into two-inch pieces, as much of the asparagus as will snap easily. That which will not snap, if fresh, will be too tough to eat. Cook it in enough salted water to barely cover the asparagus, setting the pan in a large cooker-pail of boiling water. It may be tender in one hour.

Cabbage

Cut a head of cabbage into two pieces; soak it in a large bowl of salted water for one-half hour or more. Cut it in quarters or smaller pieces, discarding the tough central stalk and any leaves which may not be perfect. Put it into four quarts of salted water to which one-fourth of a teaspoonful of baking soda has been added. Bring it to a boil and put it into a hay-box for from one and one-half to twelve hours. Winter cabbage will require three or four hours of cooking at the least. Drain it into a colander and serve it with White Sauce or with butter, pepper, and salt to taste. If cooked many hours, reheat it before serving.

Cauliflower

Soak the whole head in a large bowl of salted water for one-half hour or more. If insects are in it this will cause them to crawl out. Bring it to a boil in four quarts of boiling salted water and cook it in a hay-box from one and one-quarter to four hours. If much overcooked it will be difficult to remove the head whole. Take it out with a skimmer and serve it on a platter, pouring over it one cupful of White Sauce. A large head will require more sauce.

Cauliflower à la Hollandaise is prepared in the same way, substituting Hollandaise Sauce for White Sauce.

Cauliflower au Gratin is prepared by removing the cooked head to a baking dish, covering it with buttered crumbs and baking it until the crumbs are brown, or by covering it with grated cheese before the crumbs are added.

Carrots

Scrub and scrape carrots. (Very young carrots need not be scraped.) Cover them with boiling salted water, bring them to a boil and put them into a cooker for from one to three hours, according to the age and condition of the carrots. They will not be injured by cooking twelve hours. If old and wilted they should be soaked several hours in cold water before being prepared for cooking. When done, cut young carrots in rounds or strips, or serve them whole. Old carrots may be cut into slices before cooking. Drain away most of the water and make Sauce for Vegetables, using the remainder of the water. Or all the water may be drained off and the carrots served with butter, salt, and pepper to taste.

Corn

Husk fresh green corn, using a clean whisk-broom to remove the silk that clings to the ear. Put it into a cooker-pail, cover it with salted water, bring it to a boil and put it into the cooker for from fifty minutes to two hours. Drain it and serve it on a hot platter, covering it with a napkin.

Beets

Scrub new beets, that is, those freshly pulled. Cut off the stalks three inches from the beets, put them into four quarts or more of boiling, salted water, boil five minutes, and put them into a cooker for five hours or more. Old beets, if wilted, should be soaked till firm, and cooked as new beets. They will require six or more hours according to their age and condition. When sufficiently cooked the skin of beets will easily slip off. Remove them from the water one by one, peel and slice them. Serve them with butter, pepper, and salt. If they cool while slicing them, reheat them before serving.

Fresh Shelled Beans

Wash from one pint to one quart of fresh shelled beans, put them into three quarts of boiling salted water, to which one-fourth teaspoonful of soda has been added, boil, and put them into a hay-box for two and one-half hours. They are not injured by several hours' cooking. Drain them and add salt, pepper, and butter to taste. The exact quantity of water in which the beans are cooked is not material. They will bear a large amount, as their flavour is strong.

String Beans

2 qts. string beans
3 qts. water
3 teaspoons salt
1⁄2 teaspoon baking soda

Wash the beans, cut them into small pieces, and put them on to boil with the water, salt, and soda. Put them into a cooker for six hours. They will not be injured by cooking for ten or twelve hours. If fewer beans are to be cooked, the water must not be decreased, unless the pail of beans is full or set into a larger pail of boiling water.

Serves six or eight persons.

Lima Beans

Wash the beans and put them on to cook in boiling salted water, to each quart of which one-eighth of a teaspoonful of soda has been added. If the quantity is small, put them into a small pail set into a larger pail of water. If the whole will fill a two-quart cooker-pail it will cook without the larger pail. Put them into a cooker for one and one-half hours or more.

Dried Lima Beans

Soak the beans over night, put them to boil in at least twice their bulk of salted water. Add one-fourth teaspoonful of soda to each quart of water. Boil, and put them into a cooker for three or four hours or more. Drain, add butter, pepper, and salt, and reheat them before serving, if necessary.

Dried Navy Beans

Soak one cupful of beans over night. In the morning drain off the water, add three quarts of boiling salted water and one teaspoonful of soda. Boil, and put them into the cooker for eight hours or more. When soft, drain them and add butter, pepper, and salt to taste. Or make pork and beans of them.

Serves five or six persons.

Chard

Put a pint of water and a teaspoonful of salt into a cooker-pail. When boiling add, little by little, the well-washed chard. If, after boiling two or three minutes, there is not enough water to cover the chard, add more boiling water. If a small amount of chard is cooked the pail or pan must be set into a cooker-pail of boiling water. Put it into a cooker for three hours or more. Drain in a colander and add salt, pepper, and butter to taste. Serve with slices of hard-cooked eggs as a garnish.

One dozen stalks and leaves serve four or five persons. Many persons cook the stalks separatelyand serve them with a white sauce, using only the leaves for greens.

Spinach

Cook in the same manner as chard, allowing two hours or more in the cooker.

One peck serves six or eight persons.

Beet Greens

Cook in the same manner as chard, allowing two and one-half hours or more in the cooker. Do not remove the little beets. When cooked, cut through the greens frequently with a knife, to make them less awkward for serving.

Stewed Celery

3 cups prepared celery
1 teaspoon salt
1 qt. water

Scrub the celery with a small brush, remove the strings, cut it in one-half-inch pieces and drop it into the boiling salted water. When it is boiling, set the pail or pan into a cooker-pail of boiling water and put it into the cooker for from two to four hours or longer, depending upon the toughness of the stalks. It will not be injured by long cooking. When tender, drain it, saving one-half cupful of the water to use in making the sauce. Serve with one cupful of Sauce for Vegetables.
Serves six or eight persons.

Macaroni

1/3 lb. macaroni (1 cup broken in pieces)
1 qt. water
1 teaspoon salt

Break the macaroni into one-inch pieces. Soak it in cold water for one hour, then drain it; or cook it without soaking. Drop it into the boiling water, let it boil, and put it into the hay-box for one and one-half hours if soaked, or two hours if not soaked. Stand the pail or pan in a cooker-pail of boiling water while in the hay-box. Macaroni will break to pieces if cooked too long. When tender, drain it in a colander and serve it plain, seasoned to taste with salt and pepper, or make it into Macaroni and Cheese or Macaroni and Ham.
Serves five or six persons.

Macaroni Italienne

1 cup macaroni in one-inch pieces
1 pt. stewed and strained tomatoes
1 cup stock or water
1 medium-sized onion
4 cloves
1 small bay leaf
1 teaspoon salt
2 teaspoons sugar
1/8 teaspoon pepper
1 cup cheese, grated or shaved

92

Soak the macaroni in cold water for one hour; stick the cloves into the onion. Drain the macaroni, put it into a pan or pail, add the other ingredients, except the cheese, and, when boiling, set the pan or pail into a cooker-pail of boiling water and put it into a cooker for two hours. Remove the onion and bay leaf and add the cheese. If it cannot be served as soon as the cheese is melted, slip the pail back into the cooker.

Serves five or six persons.

Macaroni Milanaise

1 cup macaroni
1 small onion
2 cloves
1 pt. tomatoes, stewed and strained
1 cup water
1 tablespoon butter
1/2 cup grated cheese
6 sliced mushrooms
1/4 cup smoked tongue or ham, cut in strips

Break the macaroni, soak it for one hour, then drain it, and put it, with the other ingredients, except the last three, into a pan or pail. When boiling, set the pan into a cooker-pail of boiling water and put it into a cooker for two hours. Remove the onion and cloves, add the last three ingredients, and when the cheese is melted it is ready to serve. If it cannot be served at once replace it in the cooker.

Serves six or seven persons.

Spaghetti

Spaghetti may be treated in the same way as macaroni. It is a similar paste moulded into a different form. Vermicelli is also the same paste, moulded into still finer threads. It is frequently used in soups, and should be broken into short pieces and added not more than two hours before it is served, or it will become so soft as to break to pieces and lose its attractive appearance.

Noodles

Noodles are made from a richer paste than macaroni, having eggs in place of water to supply the moisture. They may be used exactly as macaroni and similar pastes. They should not be soaked before cooking.

Creamed Mushrooms

Wash the mushrooms, cut them in slices if they are large, bring them to a boil in enough salted water to nearly cover them. It should take about a pint for each quart of mushrooms. Set the pan or pail in a cooker-pail of boiling water and put it into the cooker for from two to six hours. When it is nearly time to serve them, drain the water off, reserving three-fourths of a cupful to use in making one and one-half cupfuls of Sauce for Vegetables, or White Sauce.

Fricasseed Mushrooms

Wash the mushrooms and dry them thoroughly on a towel. Let them stand on the towel some time before cooking them, so that they may drain dry. Fry them in butter till they are brown in a cooker-pail or pan, and make one and one-half cupfuls of Brown Sauce for each quart of mushrooms, using any liquor that may have come from them, and water for the liquid of the sauce. Pour this sauce over the mushrooms. If a small quantity of mushrooms is being cooked, stand the pail or pan in a large cooker-pail of boiling water. Put them into a cooker for two hours or more.

Onions

Pare onions under water, to avoid their irritating effect on the eyes. They are so strong in flavour that they will bear an excess of water in cooking. Salt the water as directed in the General Directions for Cooking Vegetables. Four quarts of water may be used for cooking one quart of onions. Bring them to a boil in a cooker-pail, and put them into a hay-box for from two hours, for very tender, fresh onions, to eight hours or more. When done, drain them dry and add butter, pepper, and salt to taste and, if desired, a little cream of milk. If the onions are very large let them boil five minutes before putting them into the hay-box.

Boiled Potatoes

Scrub potatoes well with a small scrubbing-brush. Pare them, and if they are inclined to be black when cooked, let them stand an hour or more in cold water before cooking them. Cook them in a large amount of boiling salted water in a cooker-pail. When they have boiled one minute put them into the cooker for from one and one-half to three hours, depending upon their quantity, size, and age. New potatoes will not require so long to cook as old. Large potatoes cut into pieces will cook in one hour.

Creamy Potatoes

1 qt. sliced potatoes
2 tablespoons butter
2 teaspoons salt
1/8 teaspoon pepper
3/4 pt. milk

Wash and pare the potatoes and cut them into thin slices. Four medium-sized potatoes will make a quart when sliced. Put all the ingredients together in a small cooker-pail or pan, set this in a large cooker-pail of boiling water, and when it is steaming hot, put the small utensil directly over the heat until it boils. Replace it in the pail of boiling water and set it in the cooker for one hour.

Serves four or five persons.

Stewed Potatoes

1 qt. cold, diced potatoes
2 cups milk
4 tablespoons butter
2 tablespoons flour
2 teaspoons salt
1/4 teaspoon pepper
2 tablespoons chopped parsley

Melt the butter in a small cooker-pail or pan, add the flour and blend the two evenly, then add the milk, one-third at a time; when it boils, put in the salt, pepper, and potatoes. Letthe whole reach boiling point and set it in a large cooker-pail of boiling water, unless it fills a small pail full, in which case it can be placed directly in a cooker nest which exactly fits it, and left for one hour or more.

Serves six or eight persons.

Peas

Shell young, green peas and bring them to a boil, using about one cupful of salted water for each quart of shelled peas. Put the pail or pan inside of another cooker-pail of boiling water and set all in a cooker for from one to two hours or more. Old peas may be left all night or all day in the cooker.

Rice, No. 1

1 cup rice
3 qts. water
3 teaspoons salt

Look over the rice and remove any husks or undesirable substances. Wash it by allowing cold water to run through a strainer containing the rice. Sprinkle it, gradually, into the boiling salted water in a cooker-pail. When it is boiling put it into a hay-box for one hour. There is a considerable difference in rice, and the time for cooking it will vary; but one hour will usually be found sufficient. Rice is injured by overcooking. When the rice is soft, drain it in a colander and set this in the oven, with the door open, for five minutes. Serve at once. Rice, when cooked, swells to four times its original bulk.

Serves six or eight persons.

Rice, No. 2

1 cup rice
2 to 2½ cups water
1 teaspoon salt

Look over and wash the rice as directed in the recipe for Rice, No. 1. Bring it to a boil in the salted water, and put it into a hay-box for one hour.

Serves six or eight persons.

Savoury Rice

1 cup rice
4½ cups highly seasoned stock
2 tablespoons butter

Look over and wash rice as directed in the previous recipes, bring it to a boil in the stock, with the butter, and cook it in a hay-box for one hour, standing the pail or pan that contains it in a larger pail of water, unless more than one cupful of rice is being cooked and the cooker-pail would be at least two-thirds full. Serve with a border of salted peanuts. The rice should be moist but not sticky when cooked.

Serves eight or ten persons.

Turkish Pilaf

½ cup rice
2 tablespoons chopped green sweet pepper or onion
1 cup tomatoes
1 teaspoon sugar
1¼ cups stock or water
1 tablespoon butter
1 teaspoon salt

Pick over and wash the rice, as directed in the recipe for boiled rice, No. 1. Chop the onion or pepper, discarding the seeds, and, if raw tomatoes are used, remove the skins and cut the tomatoes in pieces before measuring them. Put all the ingredients together in a small cooker-pail or pan, and, when boiling, set it in a larger cooker-pail of boiling water. Put it into a cooker for one hour. When ready to serve it, stir it lightly with a fork till all the ingredients are evenly mixed. Pilaf is injured by much overcooking.

Serves five or six persons.

Samp (Coarse Hominy)

½ cup samp
1 cup cold water
1 teaspoon salt
3 cups boiling water

Soak the samp in the cold water for eight hours or more. Add the salt and boiling water; boil it hard for one hour, and put it into a cooker for from six to twelve hours. It is improved by the longer cooking. The pail or pan in which it is cooked should be stood in a large cooker-pail of boiling water. A tablespoonful of butter may be added before serving if it is used as a vegetable.

Serves five or six persons.

Summer Squash

Scrub young, tender summer squashes and cook them whole, in the cooker, with enough salted boiling water to fully cover them, for from one to three hours. If they are not young enough to have a soft rind, they must be pared and the seeds removed. It will then be better to cook them as winter squash. When they are tender, drain off the water and mash the squashes in a colander. This will allow a little of the juice to drain away and leave the squashes drier. Season them highly with salt and pepper, and add two tablespoonfuls of butter to each pint of squash. If not very hot when mashed, reheat before serving.

Stewed Tomatoes

1 qt. tomatoes
2 teaspoons salt
1/4 teaspoon pepper
1 onion, sliced
1/4 cup buttered crumbs
2 teaspoons sugar

Scald and peel the tomatoes, remove the cores, and cut them into pieces before measuring them. Add the other ingredients, omitting the sugar and crumbs, if preferred; bring all to a boil, and put them into a cooker for from one to two hours or more. They will not be injured by indefinite cooking.

Serves five or six persons.

Hubbard or Winter Squash

Scrub, pare and cut the squash into pieces, removing the seeds. Put it into a strainer that will fit into the cooker-pail, placing a rack under it to raise it above the water in the pail. Fill the pail below the strainer with boiling water. Steam the squash directly over the fire for ten minutes, then put it into the cooker for from five to eight hours, depending upon the age of the squash and the amount cooked. A pail of not less than six quarts' capacity should be used, so that there may be at least three quarts of water under the squash. When tender, mash it through the strainer, or drain it in a cheese cloth, squeezing it as dry as possible. If it is to be served as a vegetable, season it highly with salt and pepper, and add two or three tablespoonfuls of butter to each pint of squash. If it is to be made into pies, omit these ingredients.

Pumpkin

Select a pumpkin with a soft rind, if possible. Prepare and cook it in the same manner as winter squash. It may be used as a vegetable or made into pies.

Creamed Turnips

Scrub, pare, and cut turnips into half-inch dice. Cook each

pint of prepared turnips with at least one quart of boiling salted water, in the cooker, for from one and one-half to three hours or more. When tender, drain them, reserving enough of the water to make one cupful of Sauce for Vegetables for each pint of turnips.

Mashed Turnip

Scrub and pare the turnips and cut them into pieces. Cook each pint of turnip with at least one quart of boiling salted water in the cooker for from one and one-half hours to three hours or more. When tender, drain and mash them in a colander and add to each pint one teaspoonful of salt, one-fourth teaspoonful of pepper, and two tablespoonfuls or more of butter. Serve very hot.

Italian Chestnuts

    1 qt. chestnuts
    1½ qts. water
    2 teaspoons salt

Shell and blanch the nuts by the directions given on page 123. Bring them to a boil with salted water, put them in a cooker for from two to four hours. Press them through a potato ricer or serve them whole, adding a little butter if desired. One quart of nuts will make about one pint when shelled and blanched.
Serves four or five persons.

Brussels Sprouts

    1 qt. sprouts
    2 or more qts. water
    Salt
    Pepper
    Butter

Wash the sprouts, bring them to a boil in salted water; put them into the cooker for from one to two hours, drain them and add salt, pepper, and butter to taste.
Serves six or seven persons.

XVIII

STEAMED BREADS AND PUDDINGS

GENERAL DIRECTIONS

A deep mould is best for cooking steamed breads and raised puddings, since there will be less risk of the water's boiling over into the food, and a larger amount may be used. It is important to have one that is the right size for the recipe, for if it is filled too full, the mixture might rise and push off the cover or be heavy from its pressure, and if not sufficiently full, it would be unsteady in the water. The water in the pail should come to two-thirds of the height of the mould. The mould should be not less than half-full of dough, and, generally not more than two-thirds full. If a small mould or a number of small moulds are to be used in a large cooker-pail, stand them upon a rack or similar device to raise them until there may be no difficulty in filling the cooker-pail at least two-thirds full of water. The cover as well as the mould should be greased on the inside with the same fat as that used in the dough or with butter. If a bread mould is not available, an empty baking-powder can, coffee can, or any tin can or box with straight sides which has a tight-fitting cover may be used, providing it is found by trial to be water-tight. If it leaks, it may be soldered at small expense, and may then be kept for cooking purposes only. Where a tightly covered can or box cannot be procured, an uncovered utensil could be used by tying on securely a cover of heavy, well-greased paper.

Boston Brown Bread

1 cup rye meal
1 cup graham flour
1 cup corn-meal
1 teaspoon salt
3/4 tablespoon soda
3/4 cup molasses
2 cups sour milk or
1 3/4 cups sweet milk or buttermilk

Mix and sift the dry ingredients together. Mix the liquid ingredients and add them, gradually, to the dry mixture. Put the dough into a well-buttered, one-quart brown bread mould or water-tight can of the same capacity. Stand the mould in a six-quart cooker-pail in enough warm water to come two-thirds of the way up the mould. Bring it quickly to a boil and boil it half an hour. Put it into a hay-box for five hours. It will not be spoiled by six hours in the cooker, but will not have quite such a dry crust. If sweet milk is used add one tablespoonful of cream of tartar; or omit the soda and use, instead, two tablespoonfuls of baking powder.

Serves six or eight persons.

Graham Pudding

1⁄4 cup butter
1⁄2 cup molasses
1⁄2 cup sweet milk
1 egg
11⁄2 cups graham flour
1⁄2 teaspoon baking-powder
1⁄2 teaspoon soda
1 teaspoon salt
1 cup raisins, seeded and cut in pieces

Melt the butter, add the egg, well beaten, molasses and milk. Mix the dry ingredients and add to them the liquid mixture. Pour it into a well-buttered, one-quart mould or into several smaller moulds. Do not fill them more than two-thirds full. Place the moulds on a rack in a six-quart cooker-pail of warm water, bring quickly to a boil and boil thirty minutes if the larger cans are used; fifteen minutes, if the small cans are used. Put it into the cooker for five hours. If sour milk is available, omit the baking powder and add an extra one-fourth teaspoonful of soda.

Serves six persons.

Steamed Apple or Berry Pudding

1 cup flour
2 teaspoons baking powder
1⁄4 teaspoon salt
1 tablespoon butter
3⁄8 cup milk (sweet)
4 apples cut in eighths
2 tablespoons sugar

Mix and sift the dry ingredients, cut the butter into them, or rub it in with the fingers, add the milk, cutting it in, lightly, with a knife. When the dough is barely mixed, so that no loose flour is left, toss it on a floured board and pat or roll it lightly till one-half inch thick. Spread the apples on it and roll it like a jelly roll. Carefully place it in a well-buttered, one-quart bread mould or water-tight can. Cover it tightly and stand it in at least a six-quart cooker-pail with enough warm water to come two-thirds of the way up its sides. Bring it quickly to a boil, boil thirty minutes and place it in a cooker for three hours. Serve immediately with warm apple sauce and Hard Sauce. If berries are used add one cupful to the dough, serve with berry sauce and omit the apple-sauce.

Serves five or six persons.

Suet Pudding

1/2 cup chopped suet
1/2 cup molasses
1/2 cup sour milk
11/2 cups flour
3/4 teaspoon soda
3/4 teaspoon salt
1/4 teaspoon ginger
1/4 teaspoon grated nutmeg
1/8 teaspoon ground cloves
1/2 teaspoon ground cinnamon

Mix and sift the dry ingredients and add the suet. Mix the milk and molasses and add them to the dry mixture. Put the dough into a buttered, one-quart bread mould or water-tight coveredcan, and stand it in a six-quart cooker-pail of warm water which reaches two-thirds of the way up the can. Boil it one-half hour and put into the cooker for five hours.

Serves six or eight persons.

Rich Plum Pudding

1/2 lb. raisins
1/2 lb. currants
2 oz. candied orange peel
2 oz. citron
1/4 lb. chopped suet
1 lb. stale, soft breadcrumbs (21/4 cups)
3/4 cup flour
1/4 lb. brown sugar
1/2 nutmeg, grated

½ tablespoon powdered cinnamon
⅛ teaspoon ground allspice
¼ pint brandy
4 eggs

Wash and seed the raisins; rub the currants with a little flour, then sift out the flour and allow water to run over the currants in the sieve until they are clean. Spread them on a towel and remove any stems, stones, etc., that may be among them. Let them stand, covered with a towel to keep out dust, until they are dry. Cut the orange peel and citron very fine, or put them through a food-chopper. Chop the suet or put it and the raisins through a coarse food-chopper; a trifle of the flour may be mixed with the suet before it is chopped to help to keep it from sticking to the chopping-knife. Beat the eggs till blended. Mix all the dry ingredients very thoroughly, add the eggs and then the brandy. Put the pudding into a covered, greased mould, chopping down through it a few times with the end of a knife, to be sure that it fills the mould without hollow spaces, and to avoid packing it firmly. Stand it in at least three quarts of warm water, in a cooker-pail. Heat it slowly but steadily till the water boils; let it boil one hour if the pudding is in one mould, or one-half hour if it is in two smaller moulds. Put it into the cooker for five hours. Remove it at once from the mould. If it is not to be used when first made, it may be kept several weeks, replaced in the mould and reheated before serving, by putting it in warm water, heating it to the boiling point and boiling it one-half hour or more. Serve it with brandy sauce.

Serves ten or twelve persons.

Steamed Cranberry Pudding

⅓ cup butter
⅔ cup sugar
2 eggs
2⅓ cups flour
1 tablespoon baking powder
⅓ cup milk
1 cup berries

Rub the butter till it is soft and add the sugar gradually. Separate the eggs and add the beaten yolks to the butter and sugar. Mix and sift the baking powder and flour together and add a little flour, alternately with a part of the milk, to the dough. When all is in, add the stiffly beaten whites and the berries. Put the mixture into

103

a buttered, one-quart mould, stand it in hot water and bring it, gradually, but steadily, to a boil. Let it boil one-half hour and put it into a cooker for five hours. Serve it with sweetened cream or hard sauce.

Serves six or eight persons.

Ginger Pudding

1/3 cup butter
1/2 cup sugar
1 egg
2 1/2 cups flour
3 1/2 teaspoons baking powder
1/4 teaspoon salt
2 teaspoons ginger
1 cup milk

Cream the butter, add the sugar gradually, and the well-beaten egg. Mix and sift the dry ingredients and add a little of the mixture alternately with part of the milk. When all is in, put the dough into a buttered mould, cover it, and boil it one-half hour in a large cooker-pail of water, then put it into a cooker for five hours. Serve it with Vanilla Sauce or Nutmeg Sauce.

Serves six or eight persons.

St. James Pudding

3 tablespoons butter
1/2 cup molasses
1/2 cup thick, sour milk
1 2/3 cups flour
3/4 teaspoon soda
1/4 teaspoon salt
1/4 teaspoon cloves
1/4 teaspoon allspice
1/4 teaspoon nutmeg
1/2 lb. dates, stoned and cut in pieces

Mix the molasses, melted butter, and milk and add them to the dry ingredients, which have been mixed and sifted. Add the dates and turn the dough into a buttered, one-quart mould. Boil it in a large cooker-pail of water for one-half hour and put it into a cooker for five hours. Serve with Hard Sauce.

Serves five or six persons.

Harvard Pudding

⅓ cup butter
½ cup sugar
1 egg
3½ teaspoons baking powder
¼ teaspoon salt
2½ cups flour
1 cup milk

Mix the butter and sugar, add the egg, then the dry ingredients, previously mixed and sifted together, alternating part of the dry ingredients and the milk until all are in. Turn it into a buttered, one-quart mould, boil in a large cooker pail of water for one-half hour and put it into a cooker for five hours. Serve it with warm apple sauce and Hard Sauce.

Serves six or eight persons.

Swiss Pudding

½ cup butter
⅞ cup flour
2 cups milk
Grated rind of one lemon
5 eggs
⅓ cup powdered sugar

Cream the butter, add the flour, gradually; scald the milk with the lemon rind, add it to the first mixture and cook it five minutes over hot water. Beat the yolks of eggs until they are thick, add the sugar, gradually, and combine these with the cooked mixture; cool it and cut and fold in the stiffly beaten whites of eggs. Turn it into a buttered, one-quart mould, boil it in a large cooker-pail of water for twenty minutes, then put it into a cooker for three hours.

Serves six or seven persons.

Rice Pudding

1 qt. milk
1 tablespoon butter
⅓ cup rice
⅛ teaspoon grated nutmeg
⅛ teaspoon salt
½ cup sugar

Heat the milk and other ingredients in a pudding pan over a cooker-pail of water. When the water boils, remove the pan and bring the pudding also to a boil. When it is boiling replace the pudding in the large pail of boiling water, cover and put it into the cooker for three or four hours. It may then be put into the oven for fifteen minutes and browned, although this is not necessary. This pudding may be cooked all night, but if cooked more than four hours it is not quite so creamy. Serve either hot or cold. One-half cupful of small, unbroken seedless raisins may be added to this recipe.

Serves six or eight persons.

Indian Pudding

2 cups water
1 cup molasses
1 teaspoon salt
2 teaspoons ginger
2/3 cup corn-meal
3 cups milk

Boil the water, molasses, salt, ginger, and meal together for ten minutes in a pail or pudding pan. Add the scalding milk. Bring it to a boil and set the pan in a cooker-pail of boiling water. Put it into a cooker for twelve hours. When done, brown in a hot oven. Serve with plain or whipped cream.

If fresh ground or coarse Southern corn-meal is used it may first be sifted with a coarse sieve to remove the largest particles, which will not grow soft with this amount of cooking. Granulated corn-meal will not require sifting.

Serves eight or ten persons.

Tapioca or Rice Custard

1/3 cup pearl tapioca
3/4 cup water
3 cups milk
1/2 teaspoon salt
2 eggs
1 tablespoon butter
1/2 cup sugar
1/2 teaspoon vanilla

Soak the tapioca in the water for one hour. Add the milk, sugar, butter, and salt. Set the pan in a cooker-pail of boiling water. When the milk is scalding remove the pan and let the pudding come to a boil. Replace it in the boiling water and put it into the cooker for one and one-half hours. Take it from the cooker, add the beaten eggs, replace it in the pail of hot water and stir it over the fire till it registers 165 degrees Fahrenheit, using a dairy or chemist's thermometer. Put it again into the cooker for one hour. When cold, add the vanilla.

Rice may be used instead of tapioca.

Serves six or eight persons.

Tapioca Fruit Pudding

1⁄2 cup pearl tapioca
1 qt. water
6 apples, pared and cored
3⁄4 cup sugar
1⁄8 teaspoon salt
2 tablespoons butter

Soak the tapioca one hour, bring it to a boil with the other ingredients in a two-quart pail, if that will fill the cooker "nest," or in a pudding pan to be set over boiling water. Put it into a cooker for one hour. Serve cold with cream. If it is preferred to serve the pudding warm, use only three cups of water.

Serves six or eight persons.

Chocolate Bread Pudding

1 qt. milk
1 pt. soft breadcrumbs
2 oz. or squares chocolate
2⁄3 cup granulated sugar
2 or 3 eggs
1⁄4 teaspoon salt
1 teaspoon vanilla
2 tablespoons powdered sugar

Scald the milk, add the crumbs, and soak them for one-half hour. Separate the eggs, reserving two of the whites for a meringue. Beat the three yolks and one white of egg together and mix them with half the granulated sugar. Melt the chocolate in a pudding pan set in a cooker-pail of boiling water, add the remaining half of the granulated sugar, and, gradually, the bread and milk, stirring it in well while still over the boiling water. Then add the yolks of eggs, salt, and vanilla. Stir it constantly, and cook it over the water until the pudding is 160 degrees Fahrenheit. Set the pail containing the pudding pan in a cooker for from one to two hours. When done, put it into a baking-dish suitable for serving, and cover the top with a meringue made by beating the whites of eggs till stiff, and adding the powdered sugar. Brown the meringue in a very hot oven, watching it carefully that it may not scorch. Serve warm, with cream. If preferred, two whole eggs may be used in the pudding, and in place of the meringue use sweetened, whipped cream.

Serves six or eight persons.

Queen of Puddings

1 qt. hot milk
1 pt. soft breadcrumbs
1/3 cup sugar
1/4 cup melted butter
3 eggs
1/2 teaspoon salt
1 teaspoon vanilla, or
1/4 teaspoon spice
1/2 glass jelly

Melt the butter in the milk; soak the crumbs in the milk for one-half hour; beat the yolks of three eggs and the white of one till mixed, add the sugar, salt, and spice to them. Mix all together and pour it into a pudding pan to fit in a cooker-pail of boiling water. Stir it till the pudding is 160 degrees Fahrenheit, then cover it and put it into a cooker for from one to two hours. Make a meringue as directed in the recipe for chocolate bread pudding, using the whites of two eggs and two tablespoonfuls of powdered sugar. Pour the pudding into a baking-dish for serving, spread the jelly on top and the meringue over this, and brown it in a hot oven.

Serves six or eight persons.

Steamed Cup Custard

1 qt. milk
4 eggs
1/2 cup sugar
1/2 teaspoon vanilla, or
1/8 teaspoon grated nutmeg

108

Heat the milk, beat the eggs, add the sugar and flavouring. Strain the mixture into hot custard cups, set them on a wire rack or inverted strainer or perforated pan, which is arranged in a large cooker-pail of rapidly boiling water in such a way that several quarts of water may be below the custards but not touch the cups. Cover tightly at once and set it into a cooker for one-half hour.

Serves six or eight persons.

Compote of Rice and Fruit

3/4 cup rice
33/8 cups milk
3 tablespoons sugar
1/8 teaspoon salt

Heat all together in a pan which is set into a cooker-pail of boiling water. When the water in the kettle boils, take out the pan and bring the mixture in it to a boil. Replace it in the pail and put it into the cooker for from one to three hours. Put it into a mould, and, when shaped, but while still warm, turn it out on to a serving dish. Put stewed or canned fruit on top, and pour the juice around it.

Serves six or eight persons.

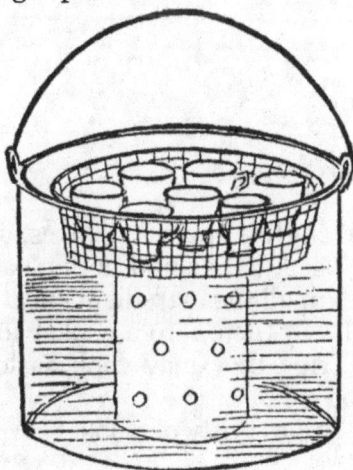

Figure No. 13
Wire rack arranged for steaming, with perforated tin can as a stand to raise it above the water.

Wire rack arranged for steaming, with perforated tin can as a stand to raise it above the water.

XIX

FRUITS

Apple Sauce

1½ qts. sour apples
1 pt. water
1 cup sugar

Wash, pare, core, and cut the apples into pieces, add the water and sugar and bring them to a boil. Put them into the cooker for from one to three hours or more, depending upon the ripeness of the apples. If they are not very tart or high-flavoured the juice of half a lemon will improve them. Apple sauce will not be harmed by indefinite cooking in the cooker. Beat it well when cooked, or, if preferred, it may be strained.

Serves six or eight persons.

Stewed Apples in Syrup

1 qt. water
½ lemon
10 cups sugar
18 cloves
10 qts. prepared apples

Pare, core, and cut tart apples in halves, unless they are small. Crab-apples may be used, but should not be pared nor cored. Wash and slice the lemon. Put all the ingredients into a cooker-pail and let them come to a boil. Put them into a cooker for three hours. If the apples are not very ripe they may cook as long as twelve hours without becoming too soft.

Serves twenty-five to thirty persons.

Apple Jelly

6 quarts prepared apples
7 cups water

Wash the apples carefully, cut them into small pieces and remove any decayed parts. Put the apples and water into a cooker-

110

pail and let them come to a boil, then set them in a cooker for four hours or more. When very soft, pour them into a jelly bag and hang this over a large bowl for several hours or over night. Measure the juice, boil it for fifteen minutes, add three quarters as much sugar as the measure of juice, boil the mixture for five minutes more, or until a drop will jelly on a cold plate if left for a few minutes. Skim the jelly carefully while it is boiling. Fruit that is slightly under-ripe is best for jelly. When cold, seal it in the following manner: For each glass cut a small piece of white paper to fit inside it, lying on the jelly. This is to be dipped into alcohol or brandy and laid in place. Cover the top of the glass with another paper cut three-fourths of an inch larger than the top of the glass, and paste it down on the sides of the glass, using white of egg or any paste without a strong odor. Or seal jelly glasses with melted paraffin poured over the top until the jelly is completely covered. Do not let the paraffin get very hot or it may give a bad flavour to the jelly.

Blackberry and Apple Jelly

    5 qts. blackberries
    2 cups water
    Apple juice

Look over the berries carefully; put them, with the water, into a cooker-pail and let them come to a boil. Put them in a cooker for three hours or more, then pour them into a jelly bag and let them drip for a least six hours. To each cupful of juice add half a cupful of apple juice prepared as for apple jelly. Boil these juices for fifteen minutes, then add five cups of sugar to each six cups of juice and boil it for five minutes longer or until a drop will jelly on a cold plate if left for a few minutes. Pour it into glasses and seal it when cold, as directed for apple jelly.

Stewed Blackberries

Pick over two quarts of berries, put them, with one cupful of sugar, into a cooker-pail and let them slowly come to a boil, stirring them occasionally as they are likely to scorch if cooked over a flame or very hot fire. When boiling, put them into a cooker for two hours or more. If cooked a very long time the juice comes out and leaves the berries rather small and seedy, but otherwise no amount of cooking hurts them.

Serves twelve or fifteen persons.

Currant Jelly

Wash twelve quarts of currants, add one cupful of water and put them on to boil. Stir them occasionally so that they will not scorch. When boiling, put them into a cooker for four hours or more. Pour them into a jelly bag and let them drip for at least six hours. Measure the juice, and when it has boiled fifteen minutes add an equal measure of sugar. Boil the mixture for five minutes, or until a few drops will jelly on a cold plate if allowed to stand a few minutes. Skim the jelly several times during the boiling. When it is done, pour it into glasses, and seal it, when cold, as directed for apple jelly.

Cranberry Jelly

1½ qts. berries
1 cup water
Sugar

Wash the berries and remove any soft and decayed ones. Bring them to a boil with the water and put them into a cooker for one or two hours or more. Mash them through a fine strainer or sieve, measure the pulp and add equal parts or three-quarters of the amount in sugar. Boil five minutes, or till a few drops will jelly on a cold plate. Pour it into moulds which have been wet with cold water. When cold, it is ready to serve.

Serves eight or ten persons.

Cranberry Sauce

1½ qts. cranberries
2½ cups sugar
1 cup water

Wash the berries and remove any that are soft and decayed. Put the berries, water, and sugar into a cooker-pail and bring them to a boil, stirring them frequently. When boiling, place the pail in a cooker for two and one-half hours or more. Serve cold.

Serves eight or ten persons.

Dried Fruits

Wash the fruit very thoroughly. If it is first soaked for five minutes and then washed, it will clean more thoroughly. To each cupful of fruit add two cupfuls of water and let it soak for at least six hours. It is better if soaked ten hours. Add the sugar and bring all to a boil. Put it into a cooker for from two to twelve hours, depending upon the fruit. Prunes are improved by long cooking, apples are not injured by it, but peaches or apricots, which are more attractive if they are not broken to pieces, will be better if removed as soon as they are perfectly soft. The amount of sugar varies for different fruits; apricots, prunelles, and such sour fruits requiring about one cupful of sugar for each pint of dried fruit; prunes, peaches, and apples requiring from one-fourth to one-half as much.

Stewed Rhubarb

1½ qts. prepared rhubarb
3/4 cup water
2 cups sugar

Wash the stalks, pare them if old, cut them into one-inch pieces and put them, with the sugar and water, into a two quart cooker-pail. When boiling, set the pail in a cooker for from one to three hours or more, depending upon the character of the rhubarb. Some people prefer to use brown sugar with rhubarb.
Serves eight or ten persons.

Stewed Figs

1 lb. figs
1½ cups sugar
Juice of one lemon
Water to cover figs

Use pulled figs; those which come in boxes crack open when they are pressed and are not so attractive when stewed. The natural form is preserved in pulled figs, and they have, besides, the advantage of being cheaper. Wash the figs and put them, with the other ingredients, into a pan which fits the cooker-pail. Boil them, set the pan in the pail of boiling water and put it into a cooker for seven hours or more. When cold, serve the figs with whipped cream.
Serves eight or ten persons.

Sweet Pickles

8 lbs. fruit (prepared)
5 lbs. brown sugar

113

1 qt. vinegar
3/8 cup stick cinnamon
3/8 cup whole allspice
1/4 cup cloves

Prepare the fruit as directed below. Tie the spices in several cheese-cloth bags, and bring them to the boiling point in a cooker-pail, with the sugar and vinegar. Add the fruit, let it barely come to a boil, stirring it carefully, so that it will not break to pieces. Set it in a cooker for the time directed below for each particular kind of fruit. When it is sufficiently cooked, remove it from the syrup and put it into cans or crocks. Boil the syrup until it loses its thin, watery consistency, and pour it over the fruit. If this occupies more than one receptacle, put one spice bag in each. Cover or seal the cans while still hot. Sweet pickles should not be eaten until they have stood for several weeks.

Peaches:

Select firm, ripe peaches, rub them well with a woolen cloth, but do not pare them. Cook them whole, as directed above, for from one to two hours or more, depending upon the hardness and size of the peaches.

Pears:

Wash, pare and, if desired, cut the pears in half, removing the cores. Cook them, as directed above, for from one to two hours or more, depending upon the hardness and size of the pears.

Crab Apples:

Wash and dry the apples and cut out the blossom. Drop them into the syrup as soon as the sugar is dissolved. Let them boil and cook them, as directed above, for from two to three hours.

Watermelon Rind or Citron:

Pare the rind and cut it into pieces. Put it into a cooker-pail of boiling salt and water, mixed in the proportion of one-half cup of salt to one gallon of water. Slip the pail at once into a cooker for ten hours or over night. When the rind is soft drain it and wash it in cold water. Drain it in a colander and add it to the syrup, prepared as directed above, and cook it, as other sweet pickles, for from four to six hours. The fruit shrinks to about one-half its bulk after cooking in the brine.

Prunes:

Soak the prunes for five minutes, wash them well, then soak them for six hours in enough water to cover them. Remove the pits, crack them, and chop the kernels. Cook the prunes and kernels in spiced syrup as directed above for ten hours or over night. Weigh the fruitafter it has been soaked in order to estimate the amount of syrup needed.

Plums:

Wipe the fruit, prick it and put it into the syrup, bring it slowly to a boil and cook it as directed above, for from one to two hours. If each plum is pricked once with a sharp-pointed fork or nut-pick it will not burst.

Quinces:

Wash the fruit and wipe it. Peel, quarter, and core it and bring it to a boil in enough water to half cover it; cook it in a cooker for ten hours or over night or steam it in a wire rack over boiling water for ten minutes and place it in a cooker for three hours; put it over the fire and bring it again to a hard boil and replace it in the cooker for another three hours. The quinces, unless very hard, will then be ready to cook in the syrup as directed above, for ten hours or over night. If they are first cooked in water instead of by steaming, the water may be used for making a syrup to use as a pudding sauce or for other purposes.

Orange Marmaláde

> 1 large grape-fruit
> 2 large oranges
> 1 large lemon
> Sugar
> Water

Wash the fruit with a brush, wipe it dry and cut it, in very thin slices, removing only the seeds. Discard the first and last slices, which consist of nothing but skin. Measure the sliced fruit, and to every quart of fruit add three cups of water. Bring it to a boil and put it into a cooker for ten hours or over night. Bring it again to a boil and cook it again for ten hours. Add the equivalent measure of both fruit and water in sugar, bring it to a boil, and put it again into the cooker for ten hours or more. If it is not sufficiently thick in consistency, boil it slowly until a drop will jelly slightly if put on a cold plate and left a few minutes. As marmalade is not usually sealed with air-tight covers it will evaporate somewhat, and become thicker by long standing, and will therefore not need to be boiled until very stiff. The longer it is boiled the less delicate the flavour becomes. This recipe should make five pints or more of marmalade.

Candied Orange or Grape-Fruit Peel

Peel of 6 oranges or 2 grape-fruit
3 cups sugar
1½ cups water in which peel was cooked

Carefully scrub the fruit till very clean, remove the peel in quarters and soak it in water for a few hours. If it is to be used as candy, scrape away a little of the white part, and cut it into very narrow strips. If to be used for cooking purposes, it need not be scraped or cut small. Put it into a cooker-pail and cover it with boiling water. Let it boil and set it in a cooker for ten hours or more. Reheat it to boiling point and cook it again for ten hours or more. This will be enough for grape-fruit, but orange-peel may require one more such period of cooking. When soft and nearly transparent, drain the peel, saving one and one-half cups of the water. Add to it three cups of sugar, and, when this is dissolved, the peel. Boil it, slowly toward the last, until most of the water has boiled away. Remove the strips and lay them in a bed of granulated sugar, covering them also with sugar. Let them stand until cold, then shake off the loose sugar, which can be used for cooking purposes, and put the candied peel into covered boxes or cans.

Canned Quinces

6 qts. quinces (prepared)
6 qts. water
4½ lbs. sugar

Wash, peel, quarter, and core the quinces before measuring them. Bring them to the boiling point with the water in a cooker-pail. When they are boiling hard put them into a cooker for ten hours or more. If they are not then very soft to the centre of the pieces, bring them again to a boil and cook them for from six to ten or more hours, according to their condition. When perfectly tender add the sugar and bring all again to the boiling point. Set them in a cooker for four hours or more. Bring them to a boil and put them at once into clean, sterilized cans. When overflowing full, seal the cans at once.

This recipe makes about eleven quarts.

Preserved Quinces

8 lbs. prepared quinces

8 lbs. sugar
2 qts. Water

Wash, peel, quarter, and core the quinces before measuring them. Put them into a cooker-pail, add the water, and when they are boiling hard, put them into a cooker for ten hours or more. If not perfectly tender, heat them again to the boiling point and set them in the cooker for as many more hours as they require, depending upon their ripeness. Thoroughly ripe quinces will probably not require this second period of cooking. Add the sugar, bring them to a boil, and set them in the cooker for four hours or more. If they are not rich enough, boil them slowly, uncovered, until they are of the desired consistency. Long, slow boiling is what gives quinces the red colour so much admired.

Citron and Ginger Preserves

6 lbs. fruit (prepared)
4 lemons
1/4 lb. green ginger
1 1/2 qts. water
6 lbs. sugar

Pare the citron and cut it into thick slices. Remove the seeds, cut the slices across into cubes, strips, or fancy shapes, and weigh them. Wash the lemons, slice them and remove the seeds. Wash and peel the ginger. Put the citron, lemon, ginger, and water into a cooker-pail. Bring them to a boil and put them into a cooker for eight hours or more, depending upon the hardness of the citron. When this is soft and nearly transparent, add the sugar, boil it, and cook again for four hours or more. Remove the fruit, put it into cans or jars, and boil down the syrup until it will just cover the fruit. Pour it at once over the fruit and close the cans when cooled. Cover them with a clean towel while cooling.

Watermelon rind may be preserved in the same manner.

Grape Jam

Remove the grapes from the stems, wash them in a colander, then press the pulp from the skins. Boil the pulp for a few minutes, until it will easily separate from the seeds. Rub it through a sieve, add the skins, and weigh or measure the mixture. Add an equal quantity of sugar, heat it over a moderate fire until it is simmering, stirring it frequently. Do not let it boil hard or the skins will be toughened. Set it in a cooker for three hours or more. Put it into sterilized glasses or jars, cover it with a towel until it is cold, and seal it as directed for apple jelly on page 110.

Grape Juice

Remove ripe Concord grapes from the stems, wash them in a colander, bring them just to the boiling point over a moderate fire, stirring them frequently. Put them into a cooker for five hours or more. Drain them in a jelly bag for at least eight hours. Each quart of loose grapes should yield about one pint of juice. Add one cup of sugar to every quart of juice; bring it just to the boiling point and pour it at once into sterilized bottles, not filling the bottles quite full. Cork them at once. When cold, press the corks down more firmly, cut them off level with the top of the bottle, and dip the inverted bottles, for an instant, into Wax for Sealing. If bubbles appear in the wax around or over the cork, break them and dip the bottle again.

Wax for Sealing Bottles

Melt together equal parts of beeswax and rosin. As soon as it is liquid it should be used or drawn back on the stove where it will not burn. It will keep indefinitely.

Preserved Ginger

Buy fresh, green ginger, of good size and quality. Peel or scrape it and cut it into lengths for serving. Cook it in a cooker for ten hours or more in boiling salted water (one-half cupful of salt to one gallon of water). Drain away the brine and add fresh boiling water to more than cover it. When boiling put it again into the cooker for ten hours or more. Change the water and cook it again, repeating this process until the ginger is very tender. It may take several days. Make a syrup, using two cupfuls of sugar to each cupful of water, bring the ginger to a boil in this syrup, set it in a cooker for five or six hours; remove the ginger, boil the syrup down to a rich consistency, and pour it over the ginger.

XX

MISCELLANEOUS RECIPES

White Sauce

2 tablespoons butter
2 tablespoons flour
1 cup milk
1/4 teaspoon salt
Few grains of white pepper

Melt the butter over moderate heat, add the flour, and blend the two thoroughly. Heat the milk over hot water, add it, one-third at a time, to the butter and flour, stirring constantly and allowing the mixture to become perfectly smooth and glossy before adding more milk. Season it and allow it to come to the boiling point. If it is not to be served immediately, cover it and slip it into the cooker to keep hot.

Sauce for Vegetables

2 tablespoons butter
2 tablespoons flour
1/2 cup of vegetable stock
1/2 cup milk
1/4 teaspoon salt
Few grains of white pepper

Make the sauce in the same manner as white sauce, blending the milk and water in which the vegetables were cooked, which is called vegetable stock.

Brown Sauce

2 tablespoons butter or clarified fat
3 tablespoons flour
1 cup brown stock
1/4 teaspoon salt
1/16 teaspoon pepper

Brown the butter slightly, add the flour and stir constantly

119

until the flour is a rich brown. Add the seasoning and stock, one-third at a time, stirring it until smooth. If butter is not used, add the flour as soon as the fat is melted, as other fats will acquire a strong flavour if allowed to brown before the flour is added. Mutton or lamb fat, or that from smoked or salted meats, is not suitable for brown sauce.

Drawn Butter Sauce

1/4 cup butter
2 tablespoons flour
1 cup boiling water
1/4 teaspoon salt
1/16 teaspoon white pepper

Melt the butter, add the flour and seasoning, and mix them well. Add the water, one-third at a time, stirring until the sauce grows smooth. When it has come to the boiling point it is done.

Caper Sauce

Drain one-half cup of capers, and add them to one cupful of drawn-butter sauce.

Egg Sauce

To one cupful of drawn-butter sauce add two hard-cooked eggs, cut in one-fourth-inch dice.

Sauce for Fish

To one cupful of drawn-butter sauce add one-half tablespoonful of lemon juice and one-half tablespoonful of chopped parsley.

Hollandaise Sauce

1/2 cup butter
Yolks of two eggs
1 tablespoon lemon juice
1/4 teaspoon salt
Cayenne pepper
1/2 cup boiling water

Rub the butter until soft and creamy, add the egg yolks, lemon juice, and seasoning, and rub them till blended, then pour on the boiling water and stand the covered bowl, containing the sauce, on a rack over a cooker pail of boiling water and put it into a cooker for three minutes; or cook it on the stove over hot water as soft custard, stirring it constantly.

Tomato Sauce

1/2 can tomatoes, or
2 cups raw tomatoes
1 slice onion
1/2 bay leaf
1 teaspoon salt
1/8 teaspoon pepper
3 tablespoons butter
3 tablespoons flour
1/2 cup water or stock

Cook all the ingredients but the butter and flour in a cooker for one hour or more. Rub them through a strainer and add this, gradually, to the blended butter and flour.

Hard Sauce

1/3 cup butter
1 cup powdered sugar
Nutmeg

Rub the butter till soft and creamy, add the sugar gradually. When perfectly blended, pile the sauce on a small dish or plate and put it into a refrigerating box or other cold place till time for serving, then grate nutmeg over the top.

Fruit Sauce

1 glass of jelly, or
1/2 pint grape juice
3/4 cup boiling water
Sugar to taste

Cut the jelly into small pieces, add the water, and bring the mixture to a boil. Let it stand in a cooker for one-half hour or more, or leave it on the stove till melted. If very sour jelly is used, some

121

sugar may be required to make it sweet enough. With grape juice about one-half cupful of sugar may be used. The sugar and water should be brought to a boil, the grape juice added, and the sauce immediately set aside to cool.

Brandy Sauce

1/4 cup butter
1 cup sugar
Yolks of two eggs
2 tablespoons brandy
1/2 cup milk or cream
Whites of 2 eggs

Warm the butter to soften, but not melt it; add the sugar gradually, and rub the two together; add the beaten yolks and, when mixed, the brandy and the milk or cream. Heat the sauce over warm water in a cooker-pail until it registers 160 degrees Fahrenheit, stirring it constantly. Cover it, and set the pail into a cookerfor twenty minutes. When it is nearly ready, beat the whites of eggs stiff and pour the hot sauce over them, beating it until it is smooth. Serve immediately.

Serves six or eight persons.

Vanilla Sauce

2 tablespoons butter
1 tablespoon flour
1 cup boiling water
1/4 cup sugar
1 teaspoon vanilla

Rub together the butter and flour in a saucepan, add the water and cook until it thickens. Add the sugar, and, when dissolved, the vanilla. Serve hot.

Nutmeg Sauce

Make it in the same way as vanilla sauce, substituting brown sugar for white, and using one-eighth teaspoonful of grated nutmeg in place of the vanilla.

Buttered Crumbs

1 tablespoon butter
1 cup soft, stale breadcrumbs
1/4 teaspoon salt
Few grains pepper

Use bread that is at least one day old, and not sufficiently stale to be hard. Grate the bread, or crumble it in the fingers; or cut it into one-inch slices, and these into quarters, and rub two quarters together. If any large pieces break off, crumble them fine with the fingers. If bread is being crumbled for scalloped dishes, it should be carefully done; if for stuffing, bread puddings, and such uses where it becomes moistened and softened it may be cut into very thin slices, then across into strips and small dice one-eighth inch in size. Mix the seasoning with the crumbs, then add them to the melted butter. When first mixed a few crumbs absorb all of the butter, but if lightly stirred with a fork for several minutes they will become evenly buttered. If richer crumbs are needed, the quantity of butter may be doubled.

Salted Nuts

1 pt. water
1/2 cup salt
1 cup blanched nuts
1 teaspoon butter

Blanch the nuts according to directions given below. Boil them in the salt and water for eight minutes, drain them and put them into a roasting-pan or pie plate with the butter. When warm, stir them well that the butter may coat each nut. Bake them in a moderate oven until they are a very light brown, stirring them frequently. When they are done, spread them out to cool and allow them to stand until crisp before putting them into a covered receptacle. If peanuts are used, take raw nuts.

To Blanch Nuts

Pour boiling water on to shelled nuts, let them stand two or three minutes, drain them and pour cold water over them. Press them from their skins.
To Shell Italian Chestnuts
Cut a slit in each nut with a sharp knife; put them into a frying

or roasting pan with one teaspoonful of butter for each pint of nuts. Shake them over moderate heat until the butter is melted, and put them into a moderate oven for five minutes; or continue to shake them over the fire for that length of time. This loosens the shell so that it may be removed with a knife.

To Sterilize Jars or Cans

Wash cans, jars or bottles and their covers and put them into a large pan of cold or tepid water, which is deep enough to fill and cover them.

Bring the water to a boil over moderate heat, unless a rack in the pan prevents contact of the glassware with the bottom of the pan, in which case a hot fire may be used. Let them boil for five minutes or more, and remove them, one by one, as they are to be filled. A clean stick or long wooden spoon-handle thrust into them may be used to take them out. Rubbers for cans should not be sterilized, as the heat will injure them. Corks may be dipped into boiling water or allowed to remain in it for a minute; but unless very stiff and shrunken, they will swell too much to fit the bottles if left long in the water.

Boiled Dressing

1 teaspoon salt
1⁄2 teaspoon mustard
Cayenne
21⁄2 teaspoons butter
1 teaspoon sugar
1 egg
1⁄2 cup milk
1⁄8 cup vinegar

Mix the dry ingredients, add the beaten egg and milk; heat them over a cooker-pail of warm water until 160 degrees Fahrenheit, stirring it constantly. Put it into a cooker for twenty minutes. Add the vinegar when it is cold, unless it is to be used for cole-slaw, in which case the hot vinegar is added at once and the dressing poured over the cut cabbage.

Soft-Cooked Eggs, No. 1

Into a cooker-pail put as many eggs as are to be cooked. Pour over them one pint of boiling water for one egg and one cup extra for each additional egg. Without heating it further, put the pail into the cooker for ten minutes. Remove them promptly at the end of that time and place them in a folded napkin to keep warm.

Soft-Cooked Eggs, No. 2

Put the eggs and cold water to more than cover them into a cooker-pail. Heat them over the fire until 165 degrees Fahrenheit, then put them into a cooker for ten minutes. Remove them immediately and serve them in a folded napkin.

Hard-Cooked Eggs

Put the eggs and enough cold water to more than cover them into a cooker-pail. Heat them till simmering, then put them into a cooker for twenty or thirty minutes, depending upon their size.

Chocolate

2 squares chocolate
1/4 cup sugar
1 cup hot water
3 cups hot milk
1/4 teaspoon vanilla

Melt the chocolate in a pan to fit over a cooker-pail of boiling water; add the salt and sugar and, when mixed, the water. Remove the pan from the pail and let the chocolate cook directly on the stove until it has thickened, add the milk, gradually, and when scalding hot, but not boiling, put the pan back into the cooker-pail of boiling water. Set all in a cooker and leave it until it is to be served. Just before serving beat it well with an egg-beater and add the vanilla. It will keep hot without injury for a number of hours and makes a good drink for a late evening supper. It can be prepared before going out and on returning from concert, theatre, or other entertainment, will be found ready to serve. A tablespoonful or two of cream improves it.

Serves four or five persons.

Cocoa

1 1/2 tablespoons cocoa
2 tablespoons sugar
2 cups boiling water
2 cups hot milk
Few grains salt

125

Mix the cocoa, sugar and salt. Mix it to a paste with boiling water, add to the remaining water, and let it boil one minute. Add the scalding milk and beat it well with an egg-beater and serve it; or put it into a cooker to keep warm until it is to be used. It will keep for several hours and should be beaten upon removal. Reception cocoa is generally made with double the quantity of cocoa and is served with a spoonful of whipped cream laid on top.

Serves four or five persons. For reception serves eight persons.

Cocoa Shells

1½ cups shells
3 cups water
3 cups milk
Sugar to taste

Bring the shells and water to a boil, put them into a cooker for eight hours or more. Add the hot milk, strain the liquid off, pressing the shells with a spoon to squeeze it out. Add the sugar and heat all until boiling. By adding one-third of a cup of cocoa nibs a more satisfactory drink is obtained. This recipe makes one quart.

Serves four or five persons.

Coffee

½ cup coffee
½ egg
Cold water
1 qt. boiling water

Mix the coffee, egg and washed shell with enough water to moisten it, in a cooker-pail or pan. Add the boiling water and let it just come to a boil. Put the pail or pan into a large pail of boiling water and set it in a cooker for one hour or more. If a larger quantity of coffee is made and it will nearly fill the cooker-pail, the outside pail of water may be omitted.

Cereal Coffee

¾ cup cereal coffee
1½ qts. Water

Put the coffee into a cheese-cloth bag and drop it into cold water. Bring it to a boil and put it into a cooker for five hours or more. It is best cooked over night and is a different thing from ordinary cereal coffee prepared by boiling. All brands of cereal coffee may be treated in this way. Serve, if possible, with cream.

Croustades

Cut stale bread into slices one and one-half or two inches thick. Cut off the crusts, making rectangular blocks of the bread, or cutting it with a large biscuit cutter, into rounds. With a fork, carefully scoop out the centres, leaving cases with walls about one-fourth of an inch thick. Brush them lightly with melted butter and brown them in a moderate oven. Creamed oysters, lobster, fish or meat and some vegetables are served in croustades.

Farina Balls

½ cup farina
2 cups milk
½ teaspoon salt
Dash of cayenne
5 drops of lemon juice
Yolk of one egg

Cook the milk and farina in a cooker for two hours or more, over boiling water, until all the liquid has been absorbed, then add the other ingredients while still over the water, and when well mixed remove it and spread it on a dish to cool. When cold, roll it into balls one inch in diameter, roll them in sifted crumbs, then in egg to which one tablespoon of water has been added and slightly beaten, and again in crumbs, and fry them in hot, deep fat until a golden brown. Drain them on soft brown paper laid on a plate in the open door of an oven. Any cold cereals may be used in this way.

XXI

RECIPES FOR THE SICK

Flaxseed Lemonade

2 tablespoons whole flaxseed
1 qt. boiling water
1/4 cup lemon juice
1/2 cup sugar
A little grated lemon rind

Pick over and wash the flaxseed in a strainer, put it into a cooker-pail and add the boiling water. When it boils put it into a cooker for from two to two and one-half hours. Strain it and add the sugar and lemon.

Farina Gruel

1 tablespoon farina
2 cups boiling water
1 tablespoon cold water
1 cup milk
1 egg
3/4 teaspoons salt

Mix the farina and cold water, add them to the boiling, salted water and when boiling set it in the cooker, over boiling water, for one and one-half hours. Then scald the milk in a double boiler and add it and the beaten egg to the cooked farina. The egg may be omitted, in which case only one cup of water should be used.

Imperial Granum

1 tablespoon Imperial Granum
1 tablespoon cold water
1/2 cup boiling water
1/4 teaspoon salt
1/2 cup milk

Mix the Imperial Granum with the cold water, add it to the boiling water. Add the salt and milk and cook it in a small cooker-pail or pan over the fire until it boils, stirring occasionally. Then put it into a pail of water and set it in a cooker for one hour or more. If preferred, more milk may be added.

Cracker Gruel

1 tablespoon plain cracker crumbs
1 cup milk
1/4 teaspoon salt

Scald the milk in a small double cooker-pail, with boiling water in the under pail. Add the cracker, and put it into a cooker for one hour or more. Add the salt just before serving. It is often convenient to keep such gruels hot for use in the night, being improved rather than harmed by the long cooking. Care must then be taken that they are hot, not merely warm. Milk is considered scalding hot when a thick skin forms on the top and bubbles appear next the pan, or when it registers 180 degrees Fahrenheit.

Oatmeal Gruel

1/2 cup rolled oats
3 cups boiling water
1 teaspoon salt
Milk to taste

Put the oatmeal, salt and water into a cooker-pan, boil it five minutes and set it in a cooker for eight or ten hours over a cooker-pail of boiling water. Rub it through a strainer, dilute it with hot milk and pour it again through a strainer.

Barley Flour Gruel

1 cup water
3 tablespoons barley flour
3 tablespoons cold water
1/2 cup milk
1/4 teaspoon salt

Mix the barley and cold water to a paste, add the boiling water and salt, bring it to a boil and cook it over boiling water for one hour or more in a cooker. Strain it, dilute it with the milk and heat it over hot water.

129

Indian Gruel

2 tablespoons meal
1 tablespoon flour
1/2 teaspoon salt
2 tablespoons cold water
3 cups boiling water
Milk or cream

Mix the flour and meal, add the cold water and add this mixture to the boiling, salted water. Boil it and let it cook over boiling water in a cooker for ten hours; strain it, add the milk or cream, heat it over hot water and serve it. Or less water may be used for the long cooking and more milk or cream be added before serving.

Arrowroot Gruel

1 cup boiling water
2 teaspoons Bermuda arrowroot
1 tablespoon cold water
1/4 teaspoon salt

Mix the arrowroot and cold water, add them to the boiling, salted water, let the mixture boil and cook it over boiling water in a cooker for one hour or more.

Pasteurized Milk

There is a certain degree of heat which, if maintained for a sufficient period of time, will destroy disease germs and certain other harmful germs which tend to spoil milk, while at the same time it is not high enough to cause the delicate flavour of raw milk to disappear. Bringing milk to this exact condition is called "pasteurizing" it. Into feeding bottles put the amount of milk that is to be used at one time. Plug them with sterilized (baked) cotton. Stand them on a rack in a cooker-pail, surrounded, to the depth of the milk, with warm water. Gradually raise the temperature till the milk in the bottles registers 150 degrees Fahrenheit. Cover the pail, and set it in a cooker for from twenty minutes to half an hour or more. Remove the bottles, cool quickly and keep the milk in a cold place, but not freezing, till needed. Do not remove the milk from the bottles if it is used for feeding infants. If used for adults do not remove it until it is to be used. Pasteurized milk will keep for a long time without souring, but is dangerous unless continuously kept very cold. Milk to be kepthot in a cooker for use in the night, should be put in while scalding hot, not merely pasteurized, since "any device for keeping milk [merely] warm should never be used."[3]

Rice and Milk

1⁄4 cup rice
11⁄4 cups milk
1⁄4 teaspoon salt

Bring the ingredients to a boil in a cooker-pan, set it over boiling water and put it into a cooker for one hour or more.

Peptonized Beef Broth

1⁄4 lb. lean beef
1 cup water
1⁄4 tube Fairchild's peptogenic powder

Remove all fat from the meat, chop it fine and heat it with the water until it boils, stirring it constantly. Drain off the liquid and grind the meat to a paste with a mortar and pestle. Put it, with the liquid and Fairchild's powder, or its equivalent, into a sterilized glass can, close it and shake all together vigorously till it is well mixed. Stand the jar with the cover laid on it, but not fastened securely, on a low rack in a cooker-pail of warm water. Place it over moderate heat until the water is 115 degrees Fahrenheit. Cover it and put it into a cooker for three hours. Warm the cooker-nest, previously, with a pail of boiling water set into it for half an hour. Take out the broth, put it into a saucepan and quickly bring it to a boil. If it is for a very sick patient it should be strained. Keep it cold unless it is used immediately. Add one-fourth teaspoonful of salt before serving it.

Peptonized Milk

1⁄2 pt. fresh milk
1⁄4 cup water
1⁄2 tube Fairchild's peptogenic powder

---

[3] "Bacteria in Milk," by L. A. Rogers. Yearbook of the Department of Agriculture, 1907, p. 194.

Put the powder with the water, which has been boiled and cooled, into a sterilized pint glass can, and shake them until the powder is dissolved. Add the milk and shake it slightly again. Put the can into a cooker-pail of warm water and heat it over a moderate fire until the water is 115 degrees Fahrenheit. Set it into a previously warmed cooker for from ten to thirty minutes. If it remains too long it will develop an unpleasant flavour. When done, remove it to a saucepan and bring it quickly to a boil. Keep it in a cold place if it is not used immediately.

Apple Water

1 large sour apple
2 teaspoons sugar
1 cup boiling water

Wash the apple thoroughly; cut it into pieces, removing the core but not the skin. Bring it to a boil in the water; cook it over boiling water in a cooker for two hours or more. Strain it through a wire strainer and add the sugar. Serve it cold.

Barley Water

3 tablespoons barley
2 cups cold water
Salt
Lemon juice
Sugar

Pick over the barley and soak it over night or for several hours. Bring it to a boil and put it into a cooker for eight hours. Strain it, add salt, sugar and lemon juice to taste. Serve it hot.

XXII

RECIPES FOR COOKING IN LARGE QUANTITIES

Fireless cookers are specially adapted to use on a large scale, as it is in cases where cooking is done on a business basis that economy in fuel, range space, and labour form such an important factor, and because there some intelligent person will generally oversee the work of the ignorant and careless. In their present form they are not, perhaps, adapted to very large institutions, where many hundreds of persons are fed, since there is a limit to the size of utensils which can be lifted in and out of the insulating box. But for small institutions, hotels, boarding-houses, restaurants, and lunch rooms the fireless cooker will, inevitably, become indispensable as soon as it is understood.

The United States Army has used the fireless cooker and, owing partly to its demand, some of the manufacturers of commercial cookers make them in sizes appropriate for use on a larges cale. For those who wish to try them without an initial outlay of much money the home-made cooker will be found in every way satisfactory. As an encouragement to those who wish to use them for such purposes, it may be said that there is less chance of failure in cooking large quantities of food than with small.

In the main, the directions for making and using cookers are the same no matter what the size, but a few points may be suggested as more necessary for large than small cookers.

In many kitchens there will be no space near the range for a cooker or a number of cookers, and it will be a matter of necessity to have one which can easily be moved. Instead of ordinary castors, use, for these, such small iron wheels as are put on hand trucks. They will be found to run more easily and to injure a floor much less. Select a box which will fit under a table, when loaded, and then it will not seem to make the kitchen any fuller than before. Fit it with two strong handles, preferably on the front of the box, so that it may be guided when pulled out from under the table.

The portable insulating pail may be found useful for transporting hot food from a central kitchen to outlying dining-rooms, as is so often done in large institutions, aluminum utensils and the lightest packing material that is practicable being advisable for these.

The temperature maintained by a large mass of food in a well-made box, will result in more rapid cooking than with small quantities, and this must be taken into account with foods, such as potatoes, which are easily overcooked.

There is always a difficulty in stating the number of persons that may be served by any recipe, since the amount served to each varies to such an extent with circumstances. The number indicated in this book is a mean between the small table d'hôte and the large à la carte portions, and is based upon the amount served at an ordinary family table. Three-quarters of a cupful is allowed for each portion of soup.

Rolled Oats

7½ qts. water
4 tablespoons salt
3 qts. rolled oats

Boil the water, add the salt and sprinkle in the oats gradually. When boiling put it into a cooker for two hours or more. It is improved by twelve hours' cooking.

Serves forty or fifty persons.

Cornmeal Mush

8 qts. water
2½ tablespoons salt
7 cups cornmeal

Mix the meal with one quart of the water, bring the remainder to a boil, add the salt and stir in the meal paste. Let it boil four minutes and put it into the cooker for five hours or more.

Serves thirty-five or forty persons.

Hominy Grits

7½ qts. water
3 tablespoons salt
1½ qts. hominy grits

Add the hominy to the boiling, salted water; let it boil for ten minutes and put it into the cooker for eight hours or more.

Serves forty or fifty persons.

Samp

   1 qt. samp
   2 qts. cold water
   3 tablespoons salt
   6 qts. boiling water

Soak the samp in the cold water for eight hours or more. Add it to the boiling water and salt, let it boil uncovered for one hour and put it into a cooker for six hours or more. A little butter added before serving improves it, if it is used as a vegetable.
Serves forty or fifty persons.

Cracked Wheat

   5 cups wheat
   2½ qts. cold water
   2½ tablespoons salt
   5 qts. boiling water

Soak the cracked wheat in the cold water for nine hours or more. Add it to the boiling water and salt, let it boil for ten minutes and put it into a cooker for at least nine hours; reheat it to the boiling point and cook it again for nine hours or more.
Serves forty or fifty persons.

Steel-cut Oatmeal

   5 cups oats
   2½ qts. cold water
   2½ tablespoons salt
   5 qts. boiling water

Cook it in the same manner as cracked wheat.
Serves forty or fifty persons.

Pettijohn's Breakfast Food

   7½ qts. water
   4 tablespoons salt
   3 qts. Pettijohn's Breakfast food

Cook it as directed on page 28.
Serves forty or fifty persons.

135

Cream of Wheat

8½ qts. water
3 tablespoons salt
5 cups cream of wheat

Cook it as directed on page 28.
Serves forty or fifty persons.

Wheatlet

Cook it in the same way as cream of wheat.

Farina

Cook it in the same way as cream of wheat.

Rice

3 to 5 qts. water
¼ cup salt
1½ qts. rice

Wash the rice, add it to the boiling salted water; let it boil and put it into a cooker for one hour.
Serves forty or fifty persons.

Brown Stock

10 lbs. meat and bone
10 qts. water
1½ teaspoons peppercorns
1 teaspoon cloves
3 bay leaves
1 tablespoon chopped thyme
1 tablespoon sweet marjoram
3 tablespoons chopped parsley
2 cups carrot
2 cups turnip
2 cups celery
1 cup onion
¼ cup salt

Make it as directed on page 31.
Serves forty-five or fifty persons.

White Stock

10 lbs. knuckle of veal
10 qts. water
1/4 cup salt
2 teaspoons peppercorns
1/2 cup onion
2 cups celery, or
1 tablespoon celery seed

Make it as directed on page 33.
Serves forty-five or fifty persons.

Mutton Broth

15 lbs. neck of mutton
10 qts. cold water
1/4 cup salt
1 teaspoon pepper
1 cup rice, or
1 cup barley

Make it as directed on page 33.
Serves forty-five or fifty persons.

Mock Turtle Soup

5 lambs' livers
5 calves' hearts
5 knuckles of veal
10 qts. water
2 cups onions
2 cups turnip
2 cups celery
1 teaspoon cloves
11/2 tablespoons peppercorns
1/4 cup salt
5 bay leaves
11/2 doz. yolks of hard-cooked eggs
21/2 lemons
Madeira wine

Make it as directed on page 36.
Serves forty-five or fifty persons.

Creole Soup

6 qts. brown stock
3 qts. tomatoes
1 cup chopped green sweet pepper
3/4 cup chopped onion
1 1/2 cups butter
2 cups flour
1 1/2 tablespoons salt
1/4 teaspoon cayenne
3/4 cup grated horseradish
2 tablespoons vinegar
1 1/2 cups macaroni rings

Make it as directed on page 38.
Serves forty or forty-five persons.

Cream of Celery Soup

3 qts. white stock
4 1/2 qts. celery, cut small
1 1/2 qts. water
1 1/2 cups sliced onion
3/4 cup butter
1 cup flour
3 qts. hot milk
1 1/2 qts. hot cream
2 tablespoons salt
3/4 teaspoon pepper

Make it as directed on page 18.
Serves forty-five or fifty persons.

Asparagus Soup

5 qts. white stock, or
5 qts. water in which asparagus has cooked
7 cans asparagus, or
7 pts. of cooked asparagus
1 3/4 cups butter

13⁄4 cups flour
31⁄4 qts. hot milk
1 tablespoon salt
3⁄4 teaspoon white pepper
1 large onion

Make it as directed on page 18.
Serves forty-five or fifty persons.

Macaroni Soup

10 qts. brown stock
21⁄2 cups macaroni rings

Make it as directed on page 39.
Serves forty-five or fifty persons.

Vegetable Soup with Stock

10 qts. brown stock
21⁄2 cups turnip
21⁄2 cups carrot
21⁄2 cups celery
21⁄2 cups cabbage
11⁄4 cups onion
1 tablespoon salt
2⁄3 cup rice or barley

Make it as directed on page 36.
Serves forty-five or fifty persons.

Ox Tail Soup

6 ox tails
9 qts. brown stock
2 teaspoons salt
1⁄4 teaspoon cayenne
1⁄2 cup butter
11⁄2 cups Madeira wine
2 tablespoons Worcestershire sauce
2 tablespoons lemon juice
Flour

Make it as directed on page 39.
Serves forty or forty-five persons.

Julienne Soup

10 qts. brown stock
2½ cups carrot
2½ cups turnip
1¼ cups peas
1¼ cups string beans
1 teaspoon salt

Make it as directed on page 39.
Serves forty-five or fifty persons.

Tomato Soup with Stock

5 qts. brown stock
5 cans or 5 qts. tomatoes
1 cup chopped onion
1¼ cups butter
1⅔ cups flour
2½ tablespoons salt

Make it as directed on page 38.
Serves forty-five to fifty persons.

Vegetable Soup without Stock

2 cups carrots
2 cups turnips
3 cups celery
3 cups onion
2 qts. potatoes
3 qts. tomatoes
1 cup butter
¼ cup chopped parsley
¼ cup salt
1½ teaspoons pepper
6 qts. Water

Make it as directed on page 40.
Serves forty-five or fifty persons.

Bean Soup

5 pts. beans
10 qts. water or stock
1 cup chopped onion
2½ lbs. lean, raw beef, if stock is not used
1 cup chopped celery
⅔ cup Chili sauce
⅔ cup butter
⅔ cup flour
¼ cup salt
1¼ teaspoons pepper

Make it as directed on page 41.
Serves fifty or fifty-five persons.

Black Bean Soup

2½ qts. black beans
10 qts. water
1 cup chopped onion
1 cup chopped celery, or
1¼ teaspoons celery salt
¼ cup salt
¾ teaspoon pepper
1¼ teaspoons mustard
¼ teaspoon cayenne
1 cup butter
½ cup flour
10 hard-cooked eggs
5 lemons

Make it as directed on page 41.
Serves fifty or fifty-five persons.

Tomato Soup

7 cans or quarts of tomatoes
3½ qts. water
1 tablespoon peppercorns
4 large bay leaves
2 teaspoons cloves
2 large onions
⅓ cup salt

1 teaspoon soda
1⁄3 cup sugar
7⁄8 cup butter
11⁄3 cups flour

Make it as directed on page 42.
Serves forty-five or fifty persons.

Potato Soup

24 medium-sized potatoes
4 qts. milk
4 qts. water
3⁄4 cup chopped onion
2 cups butter
1 cup flour
1⁄4 cup salt
2 teaspoons celery salt
1 teaspoon pepper
1⁄4 teaspoon cayenne
1⁄4 cup chopped parsley

Make it at directed on page 44.
Serves forty-five or fifty persons.

Purée of Lima Beans

5 cups dried lima beans
71⁄2 qts. water
1⁄2 cup chopped onion
3⁄4 cup chopped turnip
5 cups cream or milk
11⁄4 cups butter
2⁄3 cup flour
1⁄4 cup salt
11⁄4 teaspoons pepper

Make it as directed on page 42.
Serves forty-five or fifty persons.

Baked Bean Soup

3 qts. cold, baked beans
6 qts. water

142

½ cup chopped onion
1 cup chopped celery
1½ qts. tomatoes
½ cup butter
½ cup flour
¼ cup Chili sauce
4 teaspoons salt
½ teaspoon pepper

Make it as directed on page 43.
Serves forty-five or fifty persons.

Green Pea Soup

8 cans marrowfat peas, or
4 qts. shelled peas
5 tablespoons sugar
4 qts. water
4 qts. milk
½ cup chopped onion
1 cup butter
1 cup flour
3 tablespoons salt
1⅓ teaspoons pepper

Make it as directed on page 43.
Serves forty-five or fifty persons.

Split-Pea Soup

2 qts. split peas
8 lbs. soup bones, beef
8 qts. water
¼ cup salt
1 teaspoon pepper

Make it as directed on page 45.
Serves fifty persons.

Fish Chowder

12 lbs. cod or other firm, white fish
3 qts. potatoes, in ¾-inch dice
¾ cup sliced onion

½ cup butter
3 qts. scalded milk
¼ lb. fat salt pork
3 tablespoons salt
½ teaspoon white pepper
2 cups oyster crackers

Make it as directed on page 44.
Serves forty-five or fifty persons.

Connecticut Chowder

Make this as directed for fish chowder, substituting two quarts of stewed fresh or canned tomatoes for the milk, which may be added to the chowder before putting it into the cooker.
Serves forty-five or fifty persons.

Creamed Salt Codfish

6 lbs. codfish
12 qts. water
1½ cups butter
2 doz. eggs
3 cups milk
¾ teaspoon pepper

Cook it as directed for Creamed Salt Codfish, No. 2 on page 84.
Serves forty or fifty persons.

Codfish Balls

2 qts. raw, salt codfish, in small pieces
4 qts. potatoes, in 1-inch pieces
About 12 qts. cold water
8 eggs
¼ cup butter
1 teaspoon pepper

Cook it as directed on page 51.
Serves forty or fifty persons.

Pot Roast

12 lbs. beef from round or rump
1½ oz. beef drippings (3 tablespoons)
Flour
1 tablespoon salt
½ teaspoon pepper
1 cup carrot
1 cup turnip
1 cup onion
1 cup celery
4 bay leaves
3 qts. Water

Have the butcher bone and roll the meat, if it is from the rump. Wipe it with a damp cloth, dredge it with flour and brown it on all sides in the drippings. Wash, pare, and cut the vegetables into pieces. Put all the ingredients with the hot, browned meat, into a cooker-pail, add the water, boiling hot, let it boil for thirty minutes and put it into a cooker for nine hours or more. Before serving bring the meat to a boil, remove it, put it in a warm place, and make three quarts of brown sauce. Strain the liquor in the pail and use it for the sauce. If there is fat on the top of the liquor remove it and use it in making the sauce.

Serves fifty persons.

Brown Sauce

½ cup butter or fat
¾ cup flour
2 teaspoons salt
¼ teaspoon pepper
1 qt. stock or water

Make it as directed on page 120.
Serves sixteen or twenty persons.

Beef à la Mode

12 lbs. round of beef
¼ lb. fat salt pork
Flour
3 tablespoons salt
1 teaspoon pepper

1 cup sliced onion
1/2 teaspoon allspice
1/2 teaspoon grated nutmeg
1/2 teaspoon whole cloves
1/3 cup rendered beef fat
About 3 qts. Water

Cook it as directed on page 58, except that there need not be an outer pail of boiling water.

Serves fifty persons.

Irish Stew

5 lbs. clear meat
2 1/2 qts. potatoes, in dice
2 1/2 cups turnips, in dice
2 1/2 cups carrots, sliced
1 1/2 cups onions, sliced
2 1/2 cups celery, in pieces
3 tablespoons salt
1 teaspoon pepper
2 1/2 cups flour
1/4 cup clear fat
4 1/2 qts. Water

Cook it as directed on page 62.

Serves forty or fifty persons.

Beef Stew à la Mode

10 lbs. beef brisket
Flour
1 cup rendered fat
1 1/2 cups sliced onion
1/3 cup salt
1 teaspoon pepper
1 teaspoon ground allspice
1 teaspoon grated nutmeg
1 teaspoon whole cloves
1 lemon, sliced
Water to cover

Buy twenty-five or thirty pounds of brisket to get ten pounds of clear, lean meat. Cook it as directed on page 60.

Serves forty or fifty persons.

Boiled Dinner

8 lbs. lean, salt pork
1⁄4 pk. turnips
1⁄3 pk. beets
1 qt. carrots
5 heads cabbage
11⁄4 pks. potatoes
2 teaspoons pepper
Water to cover

Cook it as directed on page 59.
Serves forty or fifty persons.

Cannelon of Beef

6 lbs. lean meat, chopped
Grated rind 11⁄2 lemons
1⁄3 cup chopped parsley
1 doz. eggs
2 tablespoons grated onion
2⁄3 cup clear fat or butter
3⁄4 teaspoon nutmeg
3 tablespoons salt
3⁄4 teaspoon pepper
11⁄2 qts. soft breadcrumbs

Cook it as directed on page 63.
Serves forty or fifty persons.

Okra Stew

6 lbs. clear, lean mutton
2⁄3 cup clear beef fat
11⁄2 cups flour
2 cups sliced onion
3 qts. tomatoes
3 qts. okra, in pieces
3 tablespoons salt
1 teaspoon pepper
3 qts. Water

Cook it as directed on page 71.
Serves forty or fifty persons.

Creamy Potatoes

1 pk. potatoes
4 qts. milk
1/3 cup salt
1 tablespoon pepper
1 1/3 cups butter

One peck of potatoes will make about ten quarts when prepared for creamy potatoes. Melt the butter in the cooker-pail, add the milk, and, while it is heating, slice the potatoes which have been pared and soaked, for two hours or more, in cold water. As each quart of potatoes is sliced put it into the hot milk. The potatoes will thus be heated to boiling point, quart by quart. Add the seasoning. When boiling, after the last quart of potatoes has been added, put all into the cooker for one hour or more.
Serves forty or fifty persons.

Veal Loaf

5 lbs. minced veal
10 eggs
1 1/4 cups melted butter
5 cups soft breadcrumbs
3/4 teaspoon pepper
2 1/2 tablespoons salt
5/8 cup chopped parsley
5/8 cup chopped onion
1/4 lb. fat salt pork
2 1/2 teaspoons ground sage

Cook it as directed on page 75.
Serves forty or fifty persons.

Macaroni Italienne

2 qts. macaroni, in one-inch pieces
4 qts. stewed and strained tomatoes
2 qts. stock or water
8 medium-sized onions
32 cloves
4 large bay leaves
3 tablespoons salt
1/3 cup sugar

148

1 teaspoon pepper
2 qts. grated or shaved cheese

Cook it as directed on page 93.
Serves forty or fifty persons.

Turkish Pilaf

1 qt. rice
8 green sweet peppers (2 cups)
3 qts. tomatoes
2½ tablespoons salt
2 tablespoons sugar
1½ qts. water
½ cup butter

Cook it as directed on page 97, without the lower pail of water.
Serves forty-five or fifty persons.

Pork and Beans

2 qts. dried beans
1 tablespoon soda
9 qts. water
3 tablespoons salt
2 lbs. salt pork
1 cup molasses
1 tablespoon mustard
¾ teaspoon pepper
Water to half cover

Soak the beans, drain them, cook them for seven hours or more, as directed on page 91, with the nine quarts of water, soda, and salt. Drain them, add the other ingredients, and bake them till browned.
Serves forty-five or fifty persons.

Boston Brown Bread

2 qts. rye meal
2 qts. granulated cornmeal
2 qts. graham flour
⅓ cup soda
¼ cup salt

1½ qts. molasses
4 qts. thick, sour milk, or 3½ qts. Buttermilk

Mix and cook it as directed on page101. Put it into seven or eight moulds.
Serves fifty persons.

Suet Pudding

3 cups chopped suet
3 cups molasses
3 cups thick, sour milk
2¼ qts. flour
1½ tablespoons soda
1½ tablespoons salt
1½ teaspoons ginger
1½ teaspoons nutmeg
¾ teaspoon cloves
1 tablespoon cinnamon

Mix and cook it as directed on pages 101-102. Put the pudding into six moulds. Serve it with a liquid sauce.
Serves forty or fifty persons.

Rice Pudding

6 qts. milk
3 cups sugar
1 teaspoon nutmeg
1½ cups rice
¾ teaspoon salt
⅓ cup butter

Cook it as directed on page 105, except that the outer pail of water may be omitted. If served cold and not browned, omit the butter.
Serves thirty or thirty-five persons.

Indian Pudding

3 qts. water
4½ qts. milk (scalding hot)
1 qt. cornmeal
2 tablespoons salt

¼ cup ginger
1½ qts. Molasses

Mix the dry ingredients with one pint of the water, add them to the boiling water and molasses, add the milk. Let all come to a boil and put it into a cooker for ten hours or more. Put it into baking dishes and brown it, or serve it without browning, either plain or with cream.

Serves forty or fifty persons.

Chocolate Bread Pudding

6 qts. milk
3 qts. soft breadcrumbs
1 tablespoon salt
2 cups sugar
18 eggs
¾ lb. chocolate
2 tablespoons vanilla

Cook it as directed on page 107, in three pudding pans, set over cooker-pails of water.

Serves forty or fifty persons.

Stewed Apples

15 qts. prepared apples
¾ teaspoon whole cloves
7 lbs. sugar
2 lemons
1½ qts. Water

Cook them as directed on page 110.
Serves thirty-five to forty-five persons.

Apple Sauce

1 pk. sour apples
1½ qts. water
3 lbs. sugar

Cook it as directed on page 110.
Serves forty-five to fifty persons.

151

XXIII

THE INSULATED OVEN

Many women in these days will find it difficult to believe that it is possible to bake without the constant presence of fire, but our great-grandmothers were well aware that foods continued to cook in the brick ovens long after the fire in them had burned out or was raked out. The insulated oven represents an adaptation of old-fashioned ideas to new and modern conditions. Although we cannot go back to the days of brick ovens, superior as they were, in certain respects, to the portable range with its quickly fluctuating heat and great waste from radiation, yet the insulated oven will not be found impossible or very difficult to set up, and the adventurous woman will, perhaps, not be content until she has tried this development of the fireless cooker.

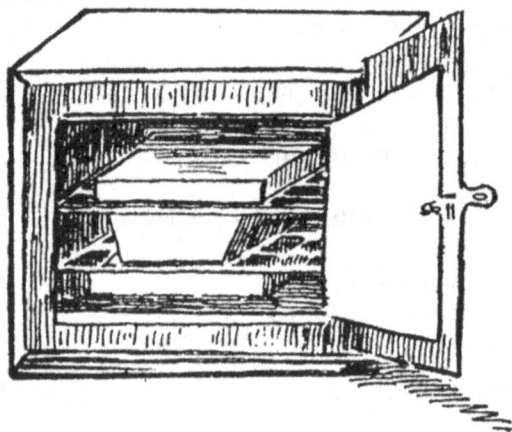

Insulated oven with stones and pan in place.

The advantages of an insulated oven lie in the even brown and thorough baking which it gives; the development and retention of flavours, which is greater than with ordinary baking; the economy in fuel where food requires long cooking; the absence of heat in the kitchen; and the possibility of baking where only a camp-fire is obtainable.

The principle is the same whether a portable oven is insulated or a cooker-pail is utilized. There must be hot stone slabs, iron plates, fire-brick, or some such heat-radiators, which can be made very hot and which will retain their heat well. Stones or fire-brick are preferable to iron in this respect. There must be insulation for

152

the oven or utensil, and cooking will then proceed, although somewhat differently from the familiar method of baking with a fire.

TO INSULATE AN OVEN

Choose as small a portable oven as will hold the food to be cooked, since the larger the oventhe larger or more numerous the stones must be to heat it. Very large stones are heavy and awkward to manage, and with their number the cost of using the oven increases. A portable oven is on the market which is about thirteen inches in each dimension. This is a good size for a family of four or five. Cut six pieces of heavy sheet asbestos, fitting one to each surface of the oven, except the door, and two to the bottom. One of the two pieces for the bottom is to go inside the oven. Place the asbestos so that it entirely covers the oven. These pieces may be tied on temporarily to hold them in place during packing. Select a box which is at least two or three inches larger in every dimension than the corresponding dimension of the oven. It should be fitted with cover and hasp just as any cooker. Lay it, while packing, with the cover opening upward. Pack in the bottom a sufficient layer of insulating material, such as is used for other cookers, to raise the oven to within a couple of inches of the top. Place the oven, lying upon its back, on this layer with the door uppermost, and opening in the same direction as the cover of the box. Pack on all sides around it till level with the door.

If desired, a facing may be made to cover the packing material, from a piece of cloth cut a few inches larger, in each direction, than the top of the box. Draw on it a square the size of the oven. In the centre of this cut a small hole to insert the blade of scissors. From this hole cut diagonally to the corners of the square. When the cloth is put in place over the packing the triangular flaps thus made may be tucked between the asbestos and the packing, while the edges of the cloth may be tucked between the packing and the sides of the box. Fit a cushion that will fill the space left at the top and nail it to the cover of the box. Face this with a piece of the sheet asbestos nailed into place. It will be well to reinforce the nail-heads with little rounds of tin, in order to prevent them from pushing through the soft asbestos. The box is then ready for use and should be stood up on end so that the cover will open like a door, and the oven will be right side up. The extra piece of asbestos may be laid in the bottom, the stones heated, and the food put in to cook.

Method of using the oven. Heat the slabs very gradually the first time that they are used. It will be best to put an asbestos mat or piece of the sheet asbestos between a hot gas flame and the stones

153

for a few minutes, not turning the gas on full force for the first five minutes. After the first using it will be safe to heat the stones directly over the flame, providing it is not burning with full force for the first few minutes. The degree of heat in the stones will regulate the heat of the oven. For most baking, the centre of the top side of the stones should be about as hot as a flatiron for ironing. This will mean that the side toward the flame is very much hotter, perhaps red hot. Another and better test is the browning of a piece of white tissue paper laid on the centre of the stones when they are put on to heat. When this grows a shade darker than manila paper, or a golden brown, the stones are right for loaf cakes, pastry, apples, potatoes, beans, scalloped dishes, most puddings, and bread. For a hot oven the paper should be a rich brown. This is suitable for biscuits, small cakes, roasting meat, etc.

Although gas is the fuel here mentioned any other fuel will serve to heat the stones, provided a hot enough flame can be procured. The stones may, when warmed, be set directly on a hot coal or wood fire to complete the heating, and, for out-of-doors use, a crude fireplace might be built up of rough stones to support the soapstones or they may be buried directly in the hot coals. In such a case it will probably be necessary to have some device, perhaps ice-tongs, for removing the stones, as the metal handles might in time become burned off, bent, or weakened so as to be unsafe.

Small soapstone griddles or foot-warmers make excellent slabs for the home-made insulated oven. Griddles are on the market that are as small as twelve inches in diameter, and foot-warmers come in many sizes. Those measuring eight by ten inches will be about as large as most women can easily handle, since they are thicker than the griddles, and are very heavy for their size. It will not be difficult to get an extra handle fitted to these, which will make them less awkward to manage. For baking many loaves of bread and cake, and for foods to cook over night, or for many hours, more than two stones may be necessary to maintain enough heat.

The oven should not be opened during the baking, but if the food is not found to be cooked when it is opened, it may be quickly closed again, and left till the food is done. A succession of articles may be baked in an already heated oven by quickly removing the finished article and one or two stones to be reheated and tested, and slipped again into place. In this case the door of the oven should be instantly closed after removing anything from it. This method of baking a number of things in quick succession is very economical as a few minutes will reheat the already warm stones.

Lay one hot stone on the asbestos at the bottom of the oven with the hotter side down; put a wire oven shelf on this, and the food on the wire shelf. If the food will not rise higher than the top of the pan, a hot stone may be laid directly across the pan, but if this is not possible place the second wire shelf as close over the food as the cleats at the side of the oven will permit, and the stone on this shelf, also with the hot side down. In case more than one pan is to go in at once, and two stones will not supply enough heat, hot flatirons or stove lids may be used to supplement them. It is often convenient, when the oven is heated for baking one article, to put other things in to cook at the same time, even though they may not require browning. For instance: A chicken or roast may be cooking between two stones, while on top of the upper stone the giblets may be stewing in water, or some vegetables be boiling. It will be best in such cases to heat these foods till boiling before putting them in the oven, or they will cool it too much. Such foods, as do not require browning, will not need another stone on top. It may not be wise to put so much watery food in the oven when baking anything so critical as bread or loaves of cake, as it cools the oven to some extent.

No matter how carefully the directions are given and followed some experimentation will probably be required before a novice, or even an experienced cook, will feel at ease with this new method of cookery, since the conditions may be so variable. But there is no reason why a careful observation of results and their causes should not soon lead one to become mistress of her own insulated oven, and it is likely that she will then become sufficiently attached to it to justify her perseverance.

In case a cooker-pail is to be utilized for baking it will be well to surround it, on top, bottom, and sides, with the heavy sheet asbestos described for insulating the oven. A wire rack will be needed for separating the food from too direct contact with the hot stones, and some device, such, perhaps, as an inverted wire frying-basket for supporting the upper stone.

LIST OF ARTICLES REQUIRED FOR MAKING AND USING AN INSULATED OVEN

Box.
Hinges.
Hasp.
Packing material, hay, excelsior, etc.
Portable oven.
Two or more stone slabs, or iron plates.
Cooking utensils, baking pans, etc.
Cloth for facing and cushion.

Nails and screws.

One dozen small rounds of tin about one inch in diameter.

One and one-quarter yards sheet asbestos (price about 20 cents a yard).

Roast Beef

Weigh the meat, trim off all parts which will not be good to serve, and save them for soups or stews. Wipe the meat clean with a damp cloth. Dredge it well with salt, pepper, and flour, put it into a dripping pan, and cook it in an insulated oven heated as directed for roasts of meat on page 153. Heat the pan and meat a little before putting them into the oven. The time for roasting beef depends upon the size and shape of the roasts. Thick pieces weighing under ten pounds will roast rare in twelve minutes to a pound, medium rare in from fifteen to eighteen minutes, and well done in twenty-five or thirty minutes a pound. Thin pieces will take a few minutes less to each pound.

Roast Mutton or Lamb

Prepare the meat for roasting as directed for roast beef. Cook it in an insulated oven heated as directed for roasts on page 153, allowing twenty-five minutes to each pound for lamb, and from fifteen to eighteen minutes for mutton.

Roast Veal

Prepare the meat for roasting as directed for roast beef. Cook it in an insulated oven, heated as for roast beef, allowing from twenty-five to thirty minutes for each pound.

Spareribs

Wipe the meat clean with a damp cloth; sprinkle it with pepper and salt, put it in a pan, and roast it in an insulated oven, heated as directed for roasts on page 153, allowing twenty minutes or more to each pound. Heat the pan and meat a little before putting it in the oven.

Brown Gravy for Roasts

Drain away all fat from the pan, leaving the brown sediment. Add to this enough water to make the desired amount of gravy. Using this in the place of stock or water make Brown Sauce, using a measured quantity of the fat from the roast. Various seasonings may be added to this sauce to make a variety. Wine, Worcestershire sauce, ketchup, currant jelly, etc., are used in this way.

Roast Chicken

Draw, stuff, and truss a chicken as directed on page 84. Put it on its back in a baking-pan, lay strips of fat salt pork on the breast, or rub breast, legs, and wings with butter or clarified veal fat. Dredge it well with salt and pepper. Heat the pan and chicken over the fire for a few minutes, and put it into an insulated oven heated as directed for roasts on page 153. Allow twenty-five minutes a pound for roasting chicken. Remove the string and skewers and serve it with Brown Gravy for Roasts to which the chopped giblets have been added. The giblets may be cooked, with salted water to cover them, in the insulated oven at the same time that the chicken is roasting; but in this case the stones should be hotter than otherwise.

Roast Goose

Singe and remove the pin-feathers from a goose. Wash it in hot, soapy water. Draw it and rinse it in cold water. Fill it two-thirds full with Stuffing for Poultry, or Potato Stuffing. Truss it, and rub the surface with butter, or lay fat salt pork on the breast. Dredge it with salt and pepper, heat it to warm the pan, and roast it in an insulated oven heated as directed for roasts on page 153, allowing fifteen or twenty minutes a pound.

Roast Leg of Venison

Prepare and cook it as roast mutton, allowing from twelve to fifteen minutes a pound for it to roast. Venison should be served rare, with Brown Gravy for Roasts, to one pint of which one-half tumbler of currant jelly and two tablespoonfuls of sherry wine have been added.

Potato Stuffing

2 cups hot potato, mashed
1 cup soft, stale breadcrumbs
¼ cup chopped salt pork
2 tablespoons chopped onion
¼ cup melted butter
⅓ cup milk
2 teaspoons salt

1 teaspoon powdered sage
1 egg

Mix the ingredients in the order given.

Roast Wild Duck

Draw, clean, and truss a wild duck in the same manner as a goose. If it is to be stuffed, use Stuffing for Poultry, omitting the herbs; or merely fill the cavity with pared and quartered apples, or pared, whole onions. These should be removed before serving, but Stuffing for Poultry should be served with the duck. Roast it for from twenty to thirty minutes in an insulated oven, the stones heated a little hotter than for other roast meats. Serve it with mashed potato and currant jelly.

Grouse

Draw and clean a grouse, remove the feathers and the tough skin of the breast. Lard the breast and legs. Truss it, and lay fat salt pork on the breast. Dredge it with salt and flour, put itinto the roasting-pan with scraps of fat salt pork. Roast it for twenty or twenty-five minutes in an insulated oven heated as for wild duck. Remove the strings or skewers, sprinkle it with browned breadcrumbs, and garnish it with parsley.

Roast Quail

Prepare the quail in the same way as grouse. Roast it for fifteen or twenty minutes in an insulated oven heated as for duck.

Roast Plover

Prepare and cook it the same as quail.

Potted Fish

3 shad or 6 small mackerel
1/3 cup salt
1/8 teaspoon cayenne pepper
1/6 cup whole cloves
1/6 cup peppercorns
1/6 cup whole allspice
1 onion, sliced
Vinegar to cover

Clean the fish, remove the head, tail, fins, skin, and large bones. The small bones will be dissolved in the vinegar. Cut the fish into pieces for serving. Mix the salt, pepper, and spices. Pack the fish in layers in a small stone crock or deep agate-ware utensil, sprinkling the salt and adding pieces of onion between the layers. Pour over it vinegar to completely cover it. In the absence of a tight-fitting cover, use heavy, buttered paper tied on. Bake it for five or six hours in an insulated oven, the stones heated until the paper test shows a delicate brown. Potted fish will keep well if put into a cold place and kept covered with vinegar. It makes a good relish for lunch or tea.

Pork and Beans

> 1 cup beans
> 1 teaspoon salt
> 1 teaspoon sugar
> 1 teaspoon molasses
> 1 tablespoon butter, or
> 1⁄8 lb. salt pork
> Water to cover

Cook the beans for four or more hours, as directed in the recipe for dried navy beans. Put them into a baking-dish, add the other ingredients, gashing the pork frequently and laying it on top. Put it into an insulated oven with stones that will turn white tissue paper a golden brown. Bake them for eight hours or more.

Baked Potatoes

Select potatoes of equal size, so that they will all bake in the same length of time; wash them and bake them in an insulated oven with the stones heated till the paper is a golden brown as explained in the test on page 153. Good-sized potatoes (eight ounces) should bake about forty-five minutes. Lay them on a rack to prevent them from touching the hot stone. They will bake better than in an ordinary oven.

Macaroni and Ham

> 1 cup macaroni, in one-inch pieces
> 1 small onion, grated
> 11⁄2 cups milk
> 2 tablespoons butter

1 tablespoon flour
1/6 teaspoon pepper
1/4 teaspoon salt
1 1/2 cups minced, cooked ham
2 cups buttered crumbs

Cook the macaroni as directed in the recipe for macaroni. Make white sauce of the milk, butter, flour, and seasoning, add the onion, ham, and macaroni. Put it into a buttered baking-dish, cover the top with the crumbs, and bake it until the crumbs are brown, heating the stones until the paper test shows a golden brown.

Serves six or eight persons.

Scalloped Oysters

1 pt. or 30 oysters
3 cups buttered crumbs
1/2 teaspoon salt
1/4 cup oyster juice
1 tablespoon finely chopped celery leaves
Few grains pepper

Wash the oysters, strain the juice through cheese-cloth. Put one-fourth of the crumbs in the bottom of a baking dish, add half the oysters, half the salt and pepper and celery leaves; repeat these layers, pour over it the oyster juice, and put the remaining crumbs on top. Bake it in an insulated oven till brown, as directed for scalloped dishes, page 153. If double this recipe is used allow three-quarters of an hour for the baking, and do not heat the stones quite so hot.

Macaroni and Cheese

1 cup macaroni in one-inch pieces
1 cup grated or shaved cheese
1/2 teaspoon salt
1/8 teaspoon pepper
2 cups buttered crumbs

Cook the macaroni in salted water as directed in the recipe for macaroni. When tender, drain it and add the salt, pepper, and cheese. Turn it into a buttered baking-dish and cover the top with the crumbs. Bake it until the crumbs are brown, heating the stones until the paper test shows a golden brown.

Serves six or seven persons.

Scalloped Chicken and Mushrooms

    2 cups buttered crumbs
    1½ cups cold, cooked chicken or fowl
    1 cup White Sauce
    1/6 teaspoon celery salt
    ½ cup mushrooms

Cut the chicken in small pieces, slice or cut the mushrooms small. Put one-fourth of the crumbs into a buttered baking-dish. Mix the other ingredients and pour them into the dish. Spread the remaining crumbs on top and bake it in an insulated oven till brown, as directed for scalloped dishes, page 153.

Scalloped Tomatoes

    1 can of whole tomatoes, or
    8 good-sized raw tomatoes
    3 cups soft breadcrumbs
    3 tablespoons butter
    1 tablespoon salt
    ¼ teaspoon pepper
    1 small onion

If canned tomatoes are used, drain away the liquid from them, using only the solid tomatoes. If raw tomatoes are used, scald them in boiling water and remove the skins and hard core. Melt the butter, add the crumbs, and stir them lightly until they are evenly buttered. Put one cupful in the bottom of a baking dish, lay the tomatoes over them, sprinkle the salt, pepper and grated onion over these and cover the top with the remaining crumbs. Bake them for one hour in an insulated oven, heating the stones until the paper test, given on page 153, shows a light brown colour.

Serves six or eight persons.

Scalloped Apples (Brown Betty)

    3 cups chopped sour apples
    2 cups soft breadcrumbs
    4 tablespoons butter

161

1/2 cup brown sugar
1/4 teaspoon cinnamon
1/4 teaspoon nutmeg
1/2 lemon, juice and rind
1/4 cup water

Melt the butter, add the crumbs, and stir them till they are evenly buttered. Mix the spice and grated rind with the sugar. Divide the buttered crumbs in quarters. Into a buttered baking dish put one-fourth of the crumbs. On this layer spread one-half the apples, then one-half the sugar. Sprinkle half of the lemon juice and water over this. Repeat these layers with one-fourth the crumbs and the remaining apple, sugar, etc. Cover the top with the crumbs that are left. Bake it for one hour and a half in an insulated oven. The stones should be heated till the test given on page 153 will show the papers a delicate brown colour. Look at the apples at the end of one hour, closing the oven after a quick glance, and alter the heat of the oven, if necessary. Serve it with Hard Sauce.

Serves five or six persons.

Rice Pudding

1 qt. milk
1/4 cup rice
1/2 cup sugar
1/8 teaspoon salt
1/8 teaspoon nutmeg

Put all the ingredients together in a baking-dish. Bake it for three hours in an insulated oven. The stones should be heated until the paper test, given on page 153, will show a light brown shade. The pudding, if correctly baked, will be creamy, with a golden brown, soft crust on top.

Serves five or six persons.

Pastry for Two Crusts

11/4 cups pastry flour
1/2 teaspoon baking-powder
1/4 teaspoon salt
1/3 or 1/2 cup butter or lard
Water

Mix and sift the dry ingredients together; cut the butter or

162

lard in with a fork. Add enough water to make a paste barely moistenough to hold together, using a knife and cutting through the dough to mix it. Roll half of it with as little pressure of the rolling-pin as possible, until it is about one-eighth of an inch thick. If a two-crust pie is to be made, lay this crust on the inside of an unbuttered pie plate, trim the edge, and put the trimmings with the remaining paste and roll it out for the upper crust. If a single under crust is to be used, as for lemon pie, lay the paste on the outside of a pie plate, trim the edge and prick through the crust in several places. Bake it for about fifteen minutes in a moderate insulated oven, with the pie plate upside down in the oven. Remove the baked crust and fill it.

Apple Pie

Sour apples
1/2 cup sugar
1 lemon, juice and rind
1/2 tablespoon butter
1/8 teaspoon cinnamon

Make pie crust by the preceding recipe, put half of it in the bottom of the plate. Pare enough apples to fill the pie heaping full, when cored and cut into eighths. Fill the pie with the apples, spread the sugar and cinnamon and grated rind over them. Roll out the upper crust, cut several gashes in it to allow steam to escape; lay it over the pie, trim the edges and press them together with a fork. Bind the edge of the pie by laying around it a wet strip of cloth about one inch wide. Bake it for one-half hour in an insulated oven with the stones heated until the paper test shows a golden brown colour.

Apple and berry pies are better made without an under crust in an extra deep pie plate.

Berry Pie

Pick over the berries. Line a deep plate with crust, or omit the lower crust; fill the pie heaping full of berries, cover them with one-half cupful or more of sugar mixed with one-fourth cupful of flour. Add the upper crust, bind it, and bake it as apple pie. The amount of sugar will depend upon the acidity of the fruit.

Cherry or Plum Pie

Wash the fruit, remove the stones, and make the pie in the same manner as berry pie.

Pumpkin Pie

1½ cups cooked pumpkin
1 cup boiling milk
1 egg
½ cup sugar
¼ teaspoon salt
⅓ teaspoon cinnamon

Cook the pumpkin as directed on page 98. Put it into a cloth and press it with the back of a strong spoon to squeeze out the water. Mix all the ingredients, put it into a pan set over a cooker-pail of boiling water; stir it until it is 165 degrees Fahrenheit, then put the whole into a cooker for one hour. Fill the baked crust with the mixture. Cover the top thickly with whipped cream.

Lemon Pie

½ cup flour
1 cup sugar, granulated
1 cup boiling water
3 tablespoons lemon juice
Rind of one lemon
4 teaspoons butter
¼ cup powdered sugar
2 eggs

Mix the sugar and flour together, add the boiling water slowly, stirring it all the time. Boil it gently for twenty minutes, stirring it frequently. Mix the lemon with the yolks, pour the hot mixture slowly on the yolks, return it to the fire and cook it below boiling point until the eggs have thickened; then add the butter. Cool the filling a little before putting it into a baked crust. Beat the whites of eggs until very stiff, add the sugar, and when barely mixed with the whites, spread it over the pie for a meringue; bake it till a delicate brown in a very hot oven, or put it for a few minutes into an insulated oven with one very hot stone close over the pie. Serve it warm, but not hot.

Serves five or six persons.

Baked Apples

Wash and core sour apples of uniform size. Put them into a pudding dish, fill the cores with sugar, and if more is desired put it into the bottom of the dish, not over the apples. Pour in enough boiling water to fill the dish one-fourth full. Bake them in an insulated oven for one-half to three-quarters of an hour, depending upon the size and ripeness of the apples. The stones should be heated until the paper test shows a golden brown colour.

Baked Spiced Apples

6 apples
30 cloves
2 cups water
2/3 cup sugar
6 slices lemon

Pare the apples, remove the cores and stick five whole cloves into each apple. Make a syrup of the water and sugar. Put the apples into a pudding dish, pour the syrup over them, and place a slice of lemon over the top of each. Bake them in a slow insulated oven for one hour with the stones heated until the paper test shows a light brown.

Baked Pears

Prepare and cook the pears as directed for baked sweet apples. If desired, a bit of butter the size of a bean may be put on each pear before baking.

Baked Quinces

Prepare and cook the quinces as directed in the recipe for baked sweet apples. Twice as much sugar and water will be required for quinces, and, perhaps, more time for baking. This will depend upon the size and ripeness of the fruit. It is usually cut in halves before baking.

Baked Sweet Apples

8 sweet apples
1/3 cup sugar
1 cup boiling water

Prepare the apples as for baked apples. Cook them in a slow insulated oven, for about three hours. The stones should be heated until the paper barely changes colour, as explained in the test given on page 153.

Bread

1 pt. water or milk
1 tablespoon butter or lard
2 teaspoons salt
2 teaspoons sugar
1/4 cake compressed or 1/2 cake dry yeast and
1/2 cup warm water, or
1/2 cup liquid yeast
Flour to make a dough

Soak the yeast for a few minutes in the half cupful of warm water. Scald the milk or boil the water, add the fat, let it cool till lukewarm, then add the remaining ingredients, except the flour. If compressed yeast is used, add as much flour as is needed to make a dough that may be kneaded. If dry yeast or liquid yeast is used, add only one and one-half pints of flour; beat the mixture well, and let it rise till full of bubbles, usually over night; then add the remaining flour. The rest of the process is the same, no matter what yeast is used. Knead the dough until it is smooth and elastic, return it to the bowl, set it in a warm place to rise until it has doubled in size. Knead it again until all large bubbles are pressed out, mould it into two loaves, put it into greased pans and let it again rise until it has doubled in size. Heat the insulated oven stones until the paper test, given on page 153, shows a golden brown. Put the bread in and bake it from fifty minutes to one hour. If two stones will not make a hot oven for a large amount of bread to be baked, use hot flatirons or stove lids to supplement them.

Rolls

Add one tablespoon of butter to the recipe for bread, or knead the butter into the dough just before moulding it. Shape it into rolls, put them into a buttered pan, and when risen to a little more than double their size, bake them for twenty minutes in an insulated oven with stones that will turn the paper a rich brown, as explained in the test on page 153.

Baking Powder Biscuits

4 teaspoons baking-powder, or
1 teaspoon soda and two teaspoons cream of tartar
1 pt. flour
1/2 teaspoon salt

2 tablespoons butter or lard
3/4 to 1 cup milk or water

Mix and sift the dry ingredients, work in the fat with the fingers, or mash it in with a fork. Add the liquid, one-third at a time, mixing the dough in three separate portions in the bowl. Cut through these three masses until they are barely mixed, then roll the dough to about one-half inch thickness; cut it into biscuits, lay them on a greased pan, brush the tops with milk or melted butter, and bake them for fifteen or twenty minutes in an insulated oven with stones heated so as to turn the paper a rich, dark brown, as explained in the test on page 153.

Cup Cake

1/2 cup butter
1 cup sugar
11/2 cups flour
2 eggs
1/2 cup milk
1/2 teaspoon nutmeg, or
1 teaspoon vanilla
11/2 teaspoons baking-powder
1/4 teaspoon salt

Cream the butter, add the sugar, then the beaten yolks of eggs. Mix and sift the dry ingredients, add them, one-third at a time, to the butter mixture, alternating with the milk. Beat the whites till stiff, add them and the vanilla, beat the dough till barely mixed, and pour it into a greased pan. The dough should not much more than half fill the pan. Bake it for forty minutes in an insulated oven, tested as explained on page 153, for loaves of cake.

This recipe may be varied by adding one-half cupful of raisins, currants, chopped citron or nuts. Or two ounces of chocolate may be melted and added to the dough.

If baked in layers or in gem pans the stones must be heated somewhat hotter than for a loaf cake. Allow fifteen or twenty minutes in the oven.

Sour Cream Cake

3 large eggs
1 cup sugar
3/4 cup thick sour cream

½ teaspoon soda
½ teaspoon baking powder
1½ cups flour
¼ teaspoon nutmeg
1 cup raisins

Beat the yolks of the eggs, add the sugar, then the cream. Mix and sift the dry ingredients, add them to the liquid mixture, then add the raisins, which have been floured with a little of the measured flour, and, lastly, the stiffly beaten whites of eggs. Put it into a greased pan and bake it for forty minutes in an insulated oven, heated for loaf cake, as explained in the test on page 153.

Apple Sauce Cake

(Made without butter, milk or eggs)

½ cup white veal or beef drippings
1 cup sugar
1 cup sour apple sauce
1½ teaspoons cinnamon
¼ teaspoon cloves
1 teaspoon nutmeg
1 cup raisins
1 teaspoon soda
2 cups flour

Mix the ingredients in the order given, beat the dough well, put it into a greased pan, and bake it for forty minutes in an insulated oven, heated for loaf cakes, as explained on page 153.

This cake seems, when baked, very much like any spice cake.

Sponge Cake

6 eggs
1 cup sugar
Juice and rind of ½ lemon
1 cup flour
¼ teaspoon salt

Beat the yolks of the eggs, add the sugar and lemon; beat the whites of eggs till stiff, add them to the mixture, and when barely mixed add the flour and salt, folding them in lightly. Put it into a bright, ungreased tin, and bake it fifty minutes or an hour in an

168

oven heated not quite so hot as for butter cakes. The paper should turn light brown when tested as explained on page 153.

Let the cake stand five minutes before removing it from the pan.

Plum Cake

1/2 cup butter
2 cups sugar
4 eggs
1/4 cup chopped nuts
1/4 cup candied orange peel
1 cup raisins
1 cup currants
5/8 cup pickled fruit syrup or molasses
2 cups flour
1/2 teaspoon soda
1/2 teaspoon cream of tartar
2 teaspoons mixed spices

Mix and sift the flour, soda, cream of tartar, and spices. Put all the ingredients together in the order given, flouring the fruit with a little of the measured flour. Put it into a greased pan and bake it for one and one-quarter hours in an insulated oven, with stones heated as explained on page 153, till the paper is a light brown.

Rich Fruit Cake

1/2 lb. butter (1 cup)
1/2 lb. sugar (1 cup)
6 eggs
1/4 cup brandy
1/4 cup lemon juice
Rind of 1 lemon, grated
2 cups blanched, chopped almonds
1/2 lb. citron
1/4 lb. candied orange peel
1 teaspoon nutmeg
1/2 teaspoon cloves
1 teaspoon cinnamon
1/2 teaspoon allspice
1 lb. raisins
1 lb. currants
1/2 lb. flour (13/4 cups)

169

Line the pan with three thicknesses of paper, buttering the top layer. Mix the flour and spices. Flour all the fruit except the citron. Mix the ingredients in the order in which they are given. The pan may be filled nearly full, as this cake rises but little. Bake it for three hours or more in a very moderate insulated oven. Test the stones as explained on page 153, until the paper will barely change colour. If, at the end of two hours, the cake is not browned at all, take out one or both of the stones very quickly and heat them again till they will slightly brown the tissue paper. The oven must be promptly closed when the stones are removed, or the cake will be injured. Test it with a steel knitting needle or straw. The needle will come out only a little greasy when the cake is done.

Let the cake stand at least five minutes after removing it from the oven before taking out of the pans, or it is likely to break. Fruit cake should be kept for at least a week in a tightly covered tin box or a crock, before it is ready for use. It will keep for months, and improves with time.

XXIV

MENUS

The planning of a menu is an art in itself. Only a knowledge of the food value of different dishes, combined with a good sense of taste and fitness, and some idea of the comparative wholesomeness of different methods of cooking, can produce a meal that is scientifically correct as well as pleasing to the palate. And now the conditions under which menus must be planned will be further modified in order to obtain the freedom from the kitchen that fireless cookery makes possible. It is thought that a classified time-table of the various dishes given in the book, giving the length of time which they require or may be allowed to cook, will be of assistance in grouping dishes that can be started at one time, put on to cook, perhaps, in one cooker, and left for the same period of time.

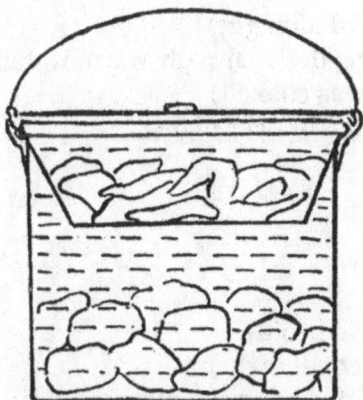

The illustration at the head of this chapter, shows a cooker-pail so arranged as to cook more than one article at once. With this arrangement a cooker with several compartments would accommodate a number of different foods at one time.

The fireless cooker makes it possible to plan a breakfast which would be ready to serve at once, or would take only a few minutes to prepare. If started in the evening, cereals may cook all night, and be entirely ready in the morning; some meat dishes may cook all night. Coffee, although better when made fresh, may be put into the cooker over night, cereal coffees being at their best after all-night cooking. With these for a basis, the menu may be varied by dishes which would cook quickly, such as eggs; or which might cook through the night and be completed in a few minutes in the morning, such as creamed codfish; or which might be cooked the day before, if served cold, such as stewed fruits; or by fresh fruits. But little of the precious early morning time would thus be required.

BREAKFASTS

No. 1

All dishes cooked over night, or served cold.
Ready to serve at once.

Apple Sauce
Oatmeal
Beef or mutton stew
Postum

No. 2

Ready to serve in fifteen minutes.

Stewed rhubarb (served cold)
Cream of Wheat (cooked all night)
Soft-cooked eggs (cooked in the morning in the already warm water
over which the cereal was cooked)
Coffee (cooked in the morning or over night)

No. 3

Ready to serve in ten minutes.

Stewed prunes (served cold)
Cornmeal mush (cooked all night)
Stewed kidney (cooked all night, finished in the morning)
Cocoa (cooked in the morning or all night)

For a midday dinner the cooker may often be filled in the morning, after breakfast, with foods requiring about three or four hours to cook, such as vegetable soup, beef stew, spinach, etc. Where a late dinner is served, it may be filled in the morning and allowed to stand all day, provided foods are chosen that need or will not be harmed by the long cooking; or it may be partly filled after breakfast and other dishes be added after lunch. Even where the entire meal is not cooked in a fireless cooker, it may be convenient to have one or two dishes so prepared, and the remainder served cold or cooked on the stove.

172

DINNERS

No. 1

To be left in the cooker three or four hours.

Creole soup
Veal cutlets
Mashed potatoes
Carrots
Stewed celery
Rice pudding

No. 2

Put into the cooker in the morning and cooked all day.

Cream of celery soup
Pot roast
Beets
Dried lima beans
Tapioca fruit pudding (previously cooked and served cold)

No. 3

Put into the cooker in the morning and cooked all day.

Mutton broth
Stuffed heart
Cabbage
String beans
Compote of rice and fruit (previously cooked and served cold)

No. 4

Part cooked all day, and part cooked through the afternoon.

Consommé
Fricasseed chicken
Samp
Winter squash
Creamed turnips
Stewed figs with cream

SUPPERS OR LUNCHES

No. 1

Hot dishes in the cooker two hours.

Breaded veal cutlets
Creamy potatoes
Stewed apricots
Cookies
Cocoa

No. 2

Hot dishes requiring only one hour to cook.

Turkish pilaf
Salmon loaf
Lettuce salad
Canned quinces
Cake
Tea

MIDNIGHT SUPPERS

Served after theatre or entertainment, the hot dish to be put into the cooker before going out. Ready to serve at once.

No. 1

Stewed oysters
Saltines
Celery
Bonbons

No. 2

Cocoa
Salad
Bread and butter sandwiches
Olives

APPENDIX

Reading references and experiments illustrating the principles upon which fireless cookery is based.

1. A test of the insulating powers of different materials.

Apparatus:

One or more boxes and fittings, described on pages 3 to 5.

One or more pails of the same size, shape and material, preferably of from two to four quarts' capacity, with close fitting covers.

Cooking thermometer
Wool
Mineral wool
Cotton batting or waste
Excelsior
Hay
Sawdust
Newspapers
Ground cork
Southern moss
Pencil
Notebook

Pack the box successively with as many of the different packing materials given above as are to be tested, following the directions given on page 7; or have several exactly similar boxes packed at the same time. For all tests fill the cooker-pail with water, bring it to the boiling point, let it boil one minute, to permit all parts of the utensil and its contents to reach the same temperature; then put it at once into the cooker-box and leave it for an equal length of time, not less than one hour. Record the temperature of the contents of the pail at the expiration of this period. In order to get a full record and a fair comparison it would be well to repeat this experiment with varying periods of time, taking the temperature, for instance, at the end of one, three, six, nine, and twelve hours. In taking temperatures do not wholly remove the cushion and cover of the pail, but slip them to one side, enough to insert the thermometer. This is, of course, a crude method of taking temperatures, but answers for purposes of comparison. If it is desired to make more accurate records this can be done by boring the cover of the box, the cushion and the pail cover, and inserting a thermometer through corks which are used to close the bored holes. The temperature can then be read while the apparatus is closed. However, the first method, if carefully done, will give probably within one degree of the correct temperature. Record the results in tabular form.

Which material do you find gives the best insulation?

Winkelmann,[4] Duff,[5] and other writers on physics give tables of the conductivity of felt, asbestos paper, paper, cotton, flannel, and other materials; but as different figures are shown, from different sources, for the same material, it is likely that the insulating power of any material used for packing a cooker will depend as much or more upon the way it is packed as upon the material used.

Experiment: Conductivity of different materials.

Take a piece of copper wire about six inches long in one hand, and a piece of steel wire of the same length and thickness in the other. Put one end of each piece in a flame, holding the wire by the extreme end. Notice which first becomes too hot to hold at the end farthest from the flame. This illustrates the different conductivity of the two materials, steel and copper. There is not a great deal of difference in the conductivity of different materials, but metals are relatively good conductors, and air is a very poor conductor.

2. *Heat is carried from the pail partly by convection, except* where solid insulating material, such as wood or indurated fibre, is used; and that manner of packing which best entangles the air and prevents air currents will, therefore, most increase the effectiveness of the insulation.

Experiment: Convection.

Into a glass flask of cold water drop a few crystals of potassium permanganate, being careful not to agitate the flask. Apply a flame to the bottom of the flask. As the water becomes heated its density is reduced and it rises, forming convection currents which are coloured by the permanganate and may be distinctly seen.

Convection currents may be formed in any liquid or gas; for instance, air. By means of them heat will be carried from one part of the liquid or gas to another. Thus air heated by contact with a kettle of food will, if allowed to flow freely, carry the heat away from the food.

3. *Heat is also lost by radiation.* This takes place less rapidly from a bright, highly polished surface, and for this reason "Thermos" and similar bottles are encased in polished nickle. A cooker-pail with polished outside surface retains heat better than one with a dull finish. In those cookers made with a metal outside

---

[4] "Hand buch der Physik."
[5] "Textbook of Physics."

retainer, the surface should not be painted or roughened or dulled by any means.

Experiment: Radiation.

Take two empty tin cans of the same size and shape. Wash off the paper labels. Keep one of them bright and shining, but move the other through a candle flame until the entire outer surface is smoked. Into each pour exactly the same quantity of water at the same temperature. Note carefully the temperature and the time. At the end of any given period, say one hour, again take the temperature of each. Which has lost the most heat, that in the bright can or that in the dull can?

4. *The effect of different degrees or thicknesses of insulation.*

Materials:

The same as those used in the experiment, section 1, with the addition of boxes of various sizes, some smaller, some larger, than the one used in the first experiment.

Pack the boxes with one or more of the various insulating materials used in the first experiment, so as to allow varying thicknesses of insulation around the cooker-pail. This should be the same or an exactly similar pail in each case. Fill the pail for all tests with an equal quantity of water, boil it for one minute, and leave it in the boxes for an equal length of time. Record the temperature maintained in each test. Keep the record in tabular form.

What thickness of insulation do you find gives the best result with the materials used in your experiment? Is it necessary to assume that the same thickness will be required with all insulating materials?

5. *The effect of the density of foods upon the temperature maintained.*

Materials:

One cooker or hay-box
Starch
Water
Salt
Cooking thermometer
Scales
Litre or quart measure
Notebook and pencil

Bring one or more litres or quarts of water to a boil, boil it for one minute, and put it into the cooker for one hour or more. Repeat the test, using, successively, five grams of salt to each litre, or one teaspoonful to each quart, and 5, 10, and 20 per cent. mixtures of

177

starch with water. Record the temperatures in tabular form, and compare the results. What would you gather to be the effect of density upon the temperatures maintained?

6. *The effect on temperature of filling the cooker-pails one-fourth, one-half, three-quarters, and entirely full.*

Materials:

Cooker or hay-box pail of eight quarts' capacity
Pail of two quarts' capacity
"Space adjuster"
Water
Thermometer
Notebook and pencil

Fill the large cooker-pail one-fourth full of water. Bring it to a boil and put it into the cooker for a definite period of time, not less than one hour. Record the resulting temperature. If desired to make the test more comprehensive, leave the water in the cooker for six, nine, or twelve hours, being careful to allow the cooker to become cold between each test. Perform the same experiment with the same pail one-half full, again when it is three-fourths full, and again when entirely full. Record the results in tabular form and compare them. Repeat these tests with a pail of two quarts' capacity. What is the influence on temperature of having pails partially, or completely, filled?

The explanation is that evaporation takes place in partially filled pails.

7. *Chemistry of the action of food materials (salt, soda, acids, water, etc.) upon cooking utensils made of tin, or aluminum, when used in a cooker or hay-box.*

The amount of tin dissolved by foods is indicated by the corrosion of the utensil, which can often be seen by the naked eye to be altered in appearance. The exact quantity of tin salts or other tin compounds which may be formed can only be determined by careful chemical analysis. It has been found that many canned goods supposed to be inert, such as squash and pumpkin, have a marked effect upon tin. Crude tests with a number of different foods can be made with tin, iron, aluminum, and copper utensils, as in many cases there is evidence to the eye of action upon the metals. It must be borne in mind, however, that such tests are crude and not decisive of the fact of there being no action in case no action is plainly visible. Only chemical analysis can prove this.

The action of foods upon tin cans bears a close relation to their action upon the utensils when used in fireless cookery, since there is time with the long cooking involved for similar reactions to take place in the cooker.[6]

Tin utensils rust badly after short use in a cooker, and thus affect the flavour of food cooked in them. This is due to the action of acids and water on the iron which forms the basis of sheet tin. When the thin plating of tin is worn off, the iron is left exposed to the action of water, etc.

Soda dissolves aluminum, and leaves a black surface on aluminum utensils. This black substance is iron, which is present with the aluminum in the utensils. To remove the black appearance, clean the utensil with acid. Do not try to remove it by scouring, as this will not do the work well, and is laborious and injurious to the pail.

Detection of poisonous metals that may be dissolved from the cooker utensils.

Experiment A. Tin. In a tin cooker-pail boil such foods as apple sauce, tomatoes, squash, or others that act on tin, and put them into a cooker for twelve hours. Transfer them to an agate ware or porcelain utensil, evaporate them over steam until they may be burned in a porcelain dish until charred and brittle. Pulverize this charred mass, and extract it with hydrochloric acid. Filter and wash it. Saturate the filtrate with hydrogen sulphide gas; add a saturated solution of potassium acetate to neutralize the hydrochloric acid present and assist in the coagulation of sulphide of tin. Warm it slightly, filter and wash out the stannic sulphide, dry it and weight it as stannic oxide, from which the tin dissolved may be calculated.

Experiment B. Aluminum.

To simplify the experiment a weak solution of malic acid may be used (seven grams per litre being about the average amount found in apples). Bring this to a boil in an aluminum cooker-pail and put it into a cooker for twelve hours. Transfer it to a porcelain vessel and add ammonia to precipitate the alumina. Filter and wash this, dry and weigh the aluminum oxide. It is probable that a smaller quantity of aluminum would be dissolved by foods of a mushy consistency than would be found in this clear solution.

8. *The efficiency of home-made refrigerating boxes compared with other means of keeping foods cold.*

Materials:

One box fitted as for fireless cooking, with two or

---

[6] See "Food Inspection and Analysis," by Leach, published by John Wiley Sons, New York, 1904, page 694.

three covered crocks of at least one-half gallon capacity, packed as directed on page 18, with either sawdust, hay, straw, excelsior or paper. Sawdust is specially recommended.

Thermometer

Ice

Notebook and pencil

Fill the central crock with a weighed quantity of ice. Fill one or both of the other crocks with water at room temperature. Cover the crocks and close the box. Record the temperature of the water at the end of six, twelve, twenty-four, and forty-eight hours.

Make repeated observations of the temperatures found in ordinary household refrigerators, cellars, cold storage rooms, and any other places used for keeping foods cold. Compare these with the temperatures obtained with a home-made refrigerating box. Is there any economy in using these boxes?

Bacteriology of Insulating Boxes

9. *Temperatures which kill disease and putrefactive germs, or check their growth.*

It is taken for granted that the student of this subject will be more or less familiar with the nature of bacteria and the elements of bacteriology. It will be recalled that bacteria are a vegetable form of life; that, like all plants, they have, under certain conditions, the power of growth which is shown, largely, by their reproduction; and that under other conditions they are killed. When their growth is merely checked, they are in a dormant state, or perhaps form spores, in either of which cases they are ready to develop as soon as their environment permits. Temperature has much to do with the state of bacteria. If the temperature and other conditions are such that they are in an active or growing state, they will multiply with enormous rapidity. When in food stuffs they effect certain changes by reason of the products which they form as a result of their life processes, or of the alteration in the food materials, owing to their abstraction of some chemical elements or compounds used for their nutrition. When bacteria form unpleasant smelling or tasting substances we speak of them as "putrefactive bacteria." Those which, if introduced into the bodies of humans or animals, will cause diseases, are called "disease bacteria." Foods are liable to contain both kinds; and, therefore, it is, obviously, wise to do all that is possible to kill them or prevent their growth.

Most forms occurring in foods grow best at from 80 degrees

to 98 degrees Fahrenheit. Few bacteria grow at above 100 degrees, and, if kept at 125 degrees, the weaker ones soon die. After subjection to a temperature of 150 degrees to 160 degrees Fahrenheit, for ten minutes, if water is present, almost all kinds are killed unless they are in the spore state. Prolonged boiling will often be resisted by spores. Dry heat is not as effective in killing bacteria as moist, and a higher temperature must, therefore, be reached to effect this end. Below 70 degrees Fahrenheit the growth of bacteria is more and more retarded, but not entirely checked until freezing point is reached. The popular idea that freezing may be relied upon to destroy bacteria is not true.

The bearing of these facts upon the subject of bacteria in foods cooked in insulating boxes is evident. Whether foods are cooked or kept cold, care must be taken that such a temperature is reached that bacteria may not grow.

In application of these principles we see that foods must be heated sufficiently to kill bacteria before it will be safe to subject them to the comparatively low temperature of the cooker for the long period necessary. This is one reason why foods in large pieces, such as roasts of meat, whole vegetables, and moulds containing a mass of food, must be boiled for a considerable time before being put into the cooker. Heat will not penetrate at once to the centre of such foods, and they would be likely to ferment or putrefy unless boiled long enough to heat the centre beyond the point where bacteria thrive. The fact that meats, cereals, and other foods have been known to sour or ferment, even after such boiling, if left in the cooker for a very long time, may be explained by the fact that, though all growing bacteria were killed, spores, which resisted the boiling, might have been present in the food, and when it cooled to a point conducive to the germination of these spores, and remained at this temperature for long, they might have developed, become active, and produced the objectionable changes characteristic of their kind.

In the case of foods to be kept in refrigerating boxes, a temperature considerably below 70 degrees Fahrenheit must be maintained. 50 degrees Fahrenheit, or lower, will be found an excellent preventive of germ growth.

Mr. L. A. Rogers has written a clear and concise description of the nature, growth, and conditions necessary to combat bacteria such as are found in food, in his paper entitled "Bacteria in Milk," published in the Yearbook of the Department of Agriculture, 1907, pages 180 to 196.

Other books which give information on this subject are "Bacteria, Yeasts, and Molds in the Home," by Conn, and "Household Bacteriology," by S. Maria Elliott.

Yeasts and moulds also may take part in the changes which spoil foods; but the temperature conditions which control bacteria would be practically the same for them.

10. *Cooking temperatures of different starches.*

Experiment: Cooking starch.

Pare and grate one or more potatoes. Wash the gratings by placing them in a cheese clothbag and immersing them in cold water. Squeeze and press the contents of the bag until no more starch seems to pass through the cloth. Let it settle, pour off the water; add clear water and let the starch settle again. Pour off the second water. Take one tablespoonful of the starch, mix it with one cupful of cold water. Heat it slowly over a moderate fire, stirring it constantly, and recording the temperature at which the mixture becomes noticeably clearer and thickens.

Repeat this experiment with corn-starch; wheat starch, washed from wheat flour, as is done with the grated potato; with starch washed from rye flour; and, if desired, with rice, bean, pea, oat and tapioca starches, also.

"Food and the Principles of Dietetics," by Hutchison, gives, on page 378, a list of different starches and the temperatures at which they gelatinize.

In a bulletin entitled "Digestibility of Starch of Different Sorts as Affected by Cooking," by Edna D. Day, Ph.D. (U. S. Dept, of Agriculture, Office of Experiment Stations, Bulletin No. 202, page 40), we read that starch takes up water at 60 degrees to 80 degrees Centigrade (140 degrees to 176 degrees Fahrenheit) and forms a sticky, colloidal substance known as starch paste, in which form it is very easily digested. Long boiling, at least to the extent of three hours, does not make it more quickly digestible.

There is something to be considered besides the mere starch in cooking starchy foods, and the fact that potato starch will form paste at 149 degrees while rice starch requires 176 degrees does not mean that less cooking will be needed for potatoes than for rice. The woody fibre or other constituents of foods, as well as their density and difference in size, must be taken into account.

11. *Cooking temperatures of proteids.*

Egg Albumen

In the bulletin entitled "Eggs and Their Uses as Food," by C. F. Langworthy, Ph.D., published as Farmers' Bulletin, No. 128, by the U. S. Department of Agriculture, the statement is made that "egg white begins to coagulate at 134 degrees Fahrenheit. White fibres appear which become more numerous until at about 160 degrees

Fahrenheit the whole mass is coagulated, the white almost opaque, yet it is tender and jelly-like. If the temperature is raised to 212 degrees Fahrenheit, and continued, the coagulated albumen becomes much harder and eventually more or less tough and horn-like; it also undergoes shrinkage. It has been found by experiment that the yolk of egg coagulates firmly at a lower temperature than the white."

It also says that these changes in the albumen suggest the idea that it is not advisable to cook eggs in boiling water in order to secure the most desirable result.

Experiment A: To show the changes that take place in egg white at various temperatures.

Materials:

> Test-tube and holder
> Beaker or saucepan of water
> Thermometer
> Egg white

Put the white of egg into the test-tube. Insert the thermometer. Hold the test-tube in the pan of cold water to the depth of the egg white. Gradually heat the water and observe the temperature at which the first change in the egg albumen takes place. Notice also the temperature of the water at this point. Continue the experiment until the water in the outer vessel has boiled ten or twenty minutes, noting the temperatures at which the various changes occur.

Experiment B: To show the temperatures obtained in the proper cooking of eggs.

Materials:

> Fireless cooker
> Eggs
> Water
> Thermometer

Cook eggs as directed for soft-cooked eggs on page 124, observing the temperature of the water after the eggs are added to it, and when they are removed from the cooker; also the condition, flavour, etc., of the eggs.

Cereal Proteids

Professor Harcourt, in his bulletin, "Breakfast Foods,"

published by the Ontario Department of Agriculture, pp. 20 and 29, says that long cooking of cereals renders the protein more digestible. The cooking which he describes was carried on in a double boiler, and, therefore, below boiling temperature, and in this respect is similar to fireless cookery. He says that while short cooking, which was done at boiling temperature, seemed to make cereal proteids less digestible, the long cooking at below boiling temperature, which followed, somewhat changed them and made them more digestible.

While little study appears to have been made of the digestibility of cereal proteids when cooked for a long time at a low temperature, it is probably fair, in the absence of further definite information, to assume that, like animal proteids, it is better to cook them at a low temperature such as that of the fireless cooker, than at the temperature of boiling water or higher.

Meat Proteids

In the bulletin entitled "A Precise Method of Roasting Meat," by Elizabeth A. Sprague and H. S. Grindley, published by the University of Illinois, a study is made of the temperatures at which the changes take place from raw meat to "rare"; from "rare" to "medium rare," and from this to "well done" meat. The authors found that if the centre of the meat is between 130 degrees and 148 degrees Fahrenheit (55 degrees and 65 degrees Centigrade), it is rare; if it is between 148 degrees and 158 degrees Fahrenheit (65 degrees and 70 degrees Centigrade), it is medium rare; and if it is between 158 degrees and 176 degrees Fahrenheit (70 degrees and 80 degrees Centigrade), it is well done. They found no advantage in cooking meat in a very hot oven (385 degrees Fahrenheit, or 195 degrees Centigrade), but rather a difficulty to keep it from burning; that in an oven which was about 350 degrees Fahrenheit (175 degrees Centigrade), the meat cooked better; and that in an Aladdin oven which kept the meat at about 212 degrees Fahrenheit (100 degrees Centigrade), it cooked best of all; that is, it was of more uniform character all through, more juicy, and more high flavoured. This seems to point to an advantage in fireless cookery for meats, and practical experience bears it out.

The initial heat of the insulated oven serves to sear and brown the meat, and when this heat is reduced by the cooling of the stones, the low temperature found to be best for completing the roasting is obtained. With regard to meats cooked in water in the cooker, experience has shown that they become well done and are more tender than when boiled, showing that the temperatures necessary to reach that degree of cooking are obtained even in the centre of a large piece of meat, without toughening or hardening the outside of the meat, as is done when more intense heat is applied.

The hardening effect of long cooking at a high temperature on meat proteids can be demonstrated by broiling a tender piece of steak until it is rare, cutting off a small piece, continuing the broiling for a few minutes, cutting off another piece and comparing these pieces with the remainder, which should be broiled until very well done.

www.ingramcontent.com/pod-product-compliance
Lightning Source LLC
LaVergne TN
LVHW030632080426
835511LV00020B/3447